United Nations peace-keeping operations

DATE DUE

JAN 0 2 2003	
APR 1 1 2005	

UNITED NATIONS PEACE-
KEEPING OPERATIONS:
A GUIDE TO FRENCH POLICIES

Edited by Brigitte Stern

*with contributions by Yves Daudet, Philippe Morillon, and
Marie-Claude Smouts*

Translated from the French by David Boyle

United Nations
University Press

TOKYO · NEW YORK · PARIS

BMR 3066 -1/1

The views expressed in this publication are those of the authors and do not necessarily reflect the views of the United Nations University.

United Nations University Press
The United Nations University, 53-70, Jingumae 5-chome,
Shibuya-ku, Tokyo 150-8925, Japan
Tel: (03) 3499-2811   Fax: (03) 3406-7345
E-mail: sales@hq.unu.edu   http: //www.unu.edu

UNU Office in North America
2 United Nations Plaza, Room DC2-1462-70, New York, NY 10017, USA
Tel: (212) 963-6387   Fax: (212) 371-9454   E-mail: unuona@igc.apc.org

United Nations University Press is the publishing division of the United Nations University.

Cover design by Joyce C. Weston

UN photo 159760/J. Isac

Printed in the United States of America

UNUP-1009
ISBN 92-808-1009-X

Library of Congress Cataloging-in-Publication Data
Vision francaise des operation de maintien de la paix. English.
    United Nations peacekeeping operations : a guide to French policies / edited by Brigitte Stern ; with contributions by Yves Daudet, Philippe Morillon, and Marie-Claude Smouts ; translated from the French by David Boyle.
      p.   cm.
    Includes bibliographical references (p.   ) and index.
    "UNUP-1009"—T.p. verso.
    ISBN 928081009X
    1. International police. 2. France—Armed Forces. 3. France—Foreign relations. I. Stern, Brigitte. II. Title.
    JZ6377.F8   V57   1998
    327.44—ddc21   98-19779
                                                   CIP

CONTENTS

PREFACE

This work is the first of what will be a series of "national guides" to peace-keeping operations (PKOs).

Conscious of the extreme importance of PKOs in the strategy of the United Nations since the first operation was set up in 1962, and particularly since the end of the Cold War and the fall of the Berlin Wall, the United Nations University considered it essential to launch a study of the subject. The originality of the approach, of which this work is an element, resides in the fact that it is not a UN analysis of PKOs, but rather an attempt to present the *national vision of peace-keeping operations* of various States.

Another unique aspect of this enterprise, which contributes to its richness, is the fact that it is not a one-dimensional analysis, considering PKOs from only one specialized angle such as law, military strategy, political science, or even their financial implications. *A multidimensional approach* has been sought in this case, and is intended to account for all the extremely diverse facets and the great complexity of peace-keeping operations.

This book deals with the French vision of peace-keeping operations as it has evolved with time. This vision takes shape through the contributions of three authors with different profiles: a researcher in political science, a law professor, and a general. All three are specialists on this question, the first two through a number of publications and the third because he has been a high-level participant of the utmost importance, deeply involved in the peace-keeping operation in Bosnia and Herzegovina.

The editor, who has had the job of coordinating the contributions, has also made a number of contributions on the subject. Any overlapping or repetition has been deliberately retained as it tends to confirm the importance of certain points. It seemed important to leave each author free to approach the subject from his or her own particular point of view, using their own personal touch and epistemo-logical references. In particular, General Philippe Morillon's presentation, which is as much a personal account as the theoretical reflection of a military strategist, appeared to add a dimension to the research that an exclusively academic work could not have attained.

The three musketeers – of whom there were in the original story four, as we all know – who set off on this adventure have taken much pleasure in it. They hope that the pleasure in the reading shall be no less.

INTRODUCTION

Brigitte Stern

The paradigm of the peace-keeping operation has become rather equivocal in recent times. There is now talk of first-, second-, and even third-generation[1] peace-keeping operations. Undeniably, between the United Nations Truce Supervision Organization in Palestine (UNTSO), created in 1948 – the first UN action which foreshadowed peace-keeping operations – and the UN involvement in the former Yugoslavia or Rwanda, peace-keeping operations have come a long way, and their image is no longer what it was.

I The various generations of peace-keeping operations

The initial peace-keeping operations – the first generation – were mainly set up to ensure peace, i.e. to silence the arms of belligerents, through interposition. Current operations – the second generation – are entrusted with much wider missions, although closely linked to rebuilding peace after conflicts. One need only glance at the Secretary-General's inventory, set out in his *Supplement to An Agenda for Peace* of 3 January 1995, to get an idea of the multiplicity of tasks now being performed by peace-keeping operations:

> the United Nations found itself asked to undertake an unprecedented variety of functions: the supervision of cease-fires, the regroupment and demobilization of

forces, their reintegration into civilian life and the destruction of their weapons; the design and implementation of de-mining programmes; the return of refugees and displaced persons; the provision of humanitarian assistance; the supervision of existing administrative structures; the establishment of new police forces; the verification of respect for human rights; the design and supervision of constitutional, judicial and electoral reforms; the observation, supervision and even organization and conduct of elections; and the co-ordination of support for economic rehabilitation and reconstruction.[2]

Today, however, just as the missions of peace-keeping operations are diversifying, the very concept of the peace-keeping operation itself is being diluted.

Indeed, as we know, peace-keeping operations were born out of the blockage of the Security Council, which was unable to act owing to the Great Power veto. The origin of the peace-keeping operation (its creation by the General Assembly) explains its main characteristics: the requirement for the consent of the State upon the territory of which it is deployed, and the founding principle of the non-use of armed force, except in cases of self-defence. These characteristics held up as long as the Security Council was operating in a political environment where the veto threatened to cause paralysis.

The international panorama changed completely after the fall of the Berlin Wall, symbolizing the end of the division of the world into two blocs. Since then, the Security Council has had its hands free, being able to set up either peace-keeping or peace enforcement operations at any time. The frontier between these two types of operations now seems to be fading, leading to the appearance of a hybrid form known as the third generation of peace-keeping operations, i.e. a peace-keeping operation based on Chapter VII of the UN Charter. UNOSOM II is the best illustration of this new type of operation, owing to the coercive nature of its mandate.

One might imagine that the two types of operations, having the same origin and mission, should be relatively interchangeable, but in fact this is not so. It must not be forgotten that, currently, they do not have the same coercive power because of differences in the make-up of their military components. Whereas peace-keeping operations are made up of lightly armed, defensive contingents, Chapter VII operations such as Desert Storm are equipped for offensive action, and often heavily armed. As the two types of operations do not address the same field operational requirements, a peace-keeping operation cannot be converted into an enforcement action without risk. The Trucy report of 1994 brings out the problem clearly:

> The role of peace-keeping and the role of peace enforcement are *two distinct roles* which cannot, be combined without giving rise to deep disillusionment. Contingents equipped for peace-keeping and humanitarian aid cannot be transformed overnight into troops called upon to fight, by a simple Security Council resolution, without compromising their security.[3]

It is for this reason that, confronted by differing operational needs, the two types of operations have been used sequentially. Such alternation was applied in Rwanda, for example, with the succession of UNAMIR I, Operation Turquoise and UNAMIR II. Even though, strictly speaking, Operation Turquoise was not a peace-keeping operation but an enforcement action under Chapter VII, things overlapped to such an extent that it appeared unreasonable to exclude Turquoise from the analysis of this book, especially since it was an operation initiated by France, conducted by France under UN authorization, and, finally, despite being based on Chapter VII, involved an intricate mixture of persuasion and coercion.

Yet another development, potentially an even greater extension of the missions of peace-keeping operations, arose out of the Declaration by the President of the Security Council at the close of the summit meeting between Heads of State and Government, on 31 January 1992:

> The absence of war and military conflicts amongst States does not in itself ensure international peace and security. The non-military sources of instability in the economic, social, humanitarian and ecological fields have become threats to peace and security.[4]

This extremely broad concept of international peace and security was elucidated in *An Agenda for Peace*, 17 June 1992:

> A porous ozone shield could pose a greater threat to an exposed population than a hostile army. Drought and disease can decimate no less mercilessly than the weapons of war. So at this moment of renewed opportunity, the efforts of the Organization to build peace, stability and security must encompass matters beyond military threats.[5]

In other words, for Boutros Boutros-Ghali, the role of the United Nations is to maintain "international security, not only in the traditional sense, but *in new dimensions presented by the era ahead.*"[6]

Thus, the emphasis has passed from peace to security. As a result, if the Security Council really wanted to implement such a concept in future, nothing could stop it from intervening, through a peace-keeping operation (or even an enforcement action), in the absence of any armed conflict, in response to a serious threat to the environment or the planet's ecological balance. This might lead to a fourth generation of peace-keeping operations, or to a change from international "peace-keeping" operations to international "security-keeping" operations ...

2   France's position: Evolving yet stable

Among all the Member States of the United Nations, France is undoubtedly the one which has had the most chequered relations with the Organization on the subject of peace-keeping operations. From being one of the countries most opposed to this new form of UN action in the 1960s, France has now become one of the principal States (if not *the* principal one) contributing to the deployment of such operations throughout the world, in the service of international peace and security.

Of course, little about the first operation, UNEF (the United Nations Emergency Force), was likely to appeal to France, either in content or form. Understandably, as an operation conducted against France, UNEF did not receive clear French support, even though France did not oppose the resolution setting it up. Furthermore, this operation could only raise French suspicions, since it was conducted following a procedure which excluded the Security Council, the role of which (along with the Great Power veto) France saw as a guarantee of its own interests and the maintenance of its international status.

Things changed with the strong French involvement in UNIFIL (the United Nations Interim Force in Lebanon) from 1978 onwards. This more positive French policy regarding peace-keeping operations has remained unchanged ever since.

So, if France has had a variable approach to peace-keeping operations, it is not so much because its position has developed in keeping with the evolution of its political interests as because peace-keeping operations themselves have changed. Specifically, French reluctance towards peace-keeping operations resulted more from the way in which they were created and conducted – by the General Assembly – than from the conception of their missions.

The most original feature of French doctrine relating to peace-keeping operations is that, unlike the Anglo-Saxon countries, France considers that *there may be a continuum between "Chapter VI and-a-half" peace-keeping operations and Chapter VII enforcement actions.* It is for precisely this reason (i.e. that a non-coercive peace-keeping operation may, at any time, become an operation using force) that France has never accepted that the General Assembly could have the power to initiate such operations.

This was the French approach from the beginning, when it considered that peace-keeping operations should only come under the control of the Security Council acting in accordance with Chapter VII, because they include various coercive aspects and, in particular, because the force's mandate may be modified in the course of the mission, passing from non-coercive action to the use of force. In the light of later deviations, such as those in the Congo and Bosnia, the premonitory nature of this French analysis must be recognized.

The French position is unchanged today. Indeed, official French doctrine with respect to peace-keeping operations seems to be based, not on the widespread dual approach distinguishing enforcement action imposed upon States from peace-keeping operations based on the consent of the parties concerned, but rather on a threefold approach:

- *peace-keeping operations*, within the framework of "Chapter VI and-a-half," maintaining peace with the consent of the parties, *in a non-conflict situation*, i.e. after the end of hostilities, or before they begin. The operations covered by this legal definition would include both the first generation of interposition operations and a certain number of preventive, or peace consolidation operations falling within the so-called second generation;
- *peace restoration operations*, conducted during an *ongoing conflict*, in a country in the throes of a civil war, where serious violations of human rights are being committed and where force may need to be used to establish peace, using a mixture of persuasion and coercion, but not against a defined aggressor;
- *peace enforcement operations*, under Chapter VII, conducted *against an aggressor*.[7]

This book may be seen as France's specific contribution to reflection on the future of peace-keeping operations.

Notes

1. This expression is used by the United Nations themselves; see United Nations Department of Press and Information [UNDPI], *United Nations Peace-keeping*, New York: UNDPI, September 1993.

2. A/50/60 - S/1995/1, para. 21, p. 6.

3. François Trucy, Senator from the Var *département*, "Rapport au Premier Ministre: Participation de la France aux opérations de maintien de la paix" [Report to the Prime Minister: France's participation in peace-keeping operations] (February 1994, mimeo), pp. 16–17. Author's emphasis.

4. S/PV/3046, p. 143.

5. A/47/277 - S/24111, para. 13.

6. *Idem*, para. 22, emphasis added.

7. B. Stern, "L'évolution du rôle des Nations Unies dans le maintien de la paix et de la sécurité internationales" [The evolution of the role of the United Nations in the maintenance of international peace and security], in *Le droit international comme langage des relations internationales* [International law as a language for international relations], Proceedings of the United Nations Congress on Public International Law, New York, 13–17 March 1995 (La Haye: Kluwer, 1996), pp. 58–64. See also the contributions of M.C. Smouts and Y. Daudet to the present volume (chapters 1–3).

1

POLITICAL ASPECTS OF PEACE-KEEPING OPERATIONS

Marie-Claude Smouts

France is an old country, laden with history, which cannot resign itself to no longer being a major power. It prides itself on being the world's fourth largest commercial power and Western Europe's major military power. Its overseas Territories and Departments[1] give it a vast maritime zone which justifies its presence on all the world's seas. Owing to its very close relations with the French-speaking countries of Africa, it is not surprising when the French army is dispatched to re-establish internal order in one or another of them. France's position at the centre of Western Europe and the strength of its links with Germany make it an essential pillar of the European edifice. All of these special factors lead to a cult of "rank" and a "French exception," bequeathed by General de Gaulle and maintained by his successors. France, "because it is France," claims to have a global vocation. It must express itself on, and intervene in, world affairs. The worst criticism the French can make of their leaders' foreign policy is not that it is expensive and hazardous, but that it is flat and lacking in style.

Against the background of such a political culture, France's seat as a Permanent Member of the Security Council is clearly a precious asset. It is a seat which was won in 1944 after a hard-fought struggle thanks to the support of Great Britain, despite Roosevelt's wariness and Stalin's disdain; a seat which is some-

times put in question when, from time to time, the vague desire for Security
Council reform raises its head; a seat which is under little threat, in reality,
but of which France must show itself worthy. France counts on its exemplary
behaviour to justify the status of great world power conferred by its membership
of the "P5" group (the five permanent members of the Security Council, in UN
jargon). It sends its best diplomats to the United Nations. It participates in all the
discussions. It pays its financial contributions. It is one of the major contributors
of troops to United Nations service. In other words, it plays the game. The policy
is simple: encourage anything capable of strengthening the prestige and the
means of action of the Security Council and, through it, France's own international influence.

France's participation in peace-keeping operations is not part of some abstract
logic of collective security. It serves material and immaterial aims of national
interest such as security imperatives, self-image, and international prestige. The
image of a grand and generous France, daughter of the Revolution and homeland
of human rights, is part of the national heritage. The quest for some "great
design" is a political necessity. In colonial times, this gave the "civilizing mission"; after colonial independence, the "North-South" policy. As the century
draws to a close, the projection of French forces into foreign theatres of operations in the name of the international community is part of a new great design:
"espouse 'just causes,' give aid and assistance to suffering populations, soothe
conflicts, and prepare for their peaceful resolution."[2]

I   The historical background

Difficult beginnings

During the first twenty years of the United Nations, relations between France
and the Organization were difficult. From 1945 to 1965, the French position on
peace-keeping activities was dominated by the converging constraints of the
Cold War and colonial conflicts. France was the only permanent member of the
Security Council racked by both of the major questions of the immediate after-
war period, the East-West conflict and decolonization.[3] France's room to
manoeuvre in the universal Organization was significantly reduced by the combined effects of a very strong French Communist Party, supported by Moscow
and gaining up to 25 per cent of the vote, and the explosion of nationalism in its

overseas possessions. In so far as the United Nations participated in the defence of the "free world," France could only be supportive. In fact, it availed itself of the United Nations as a platform from which to flay communism and denounce the human rights situation in the Eastern bloc countries. At the same time, however, the price paid for Western solidarity under the absolute domination of the United States was a gradual loss of power which, through procedural device, displaced the United Nations' decision-making centre from the Security Council to the General Assembly and the Secretariat. Not only did this bending of the UN Charter eat into France's prerogatives as a permanent member of the Security Council, but it also exposed the country to having its internal affairs submitted to the critical attention of the United Nations, when, in fact, the aim of the greater part of France's diplomatic activity was precisely to keep its colonial affairs out of the UN forum so as to avoid any unfavourable vote on North African questions. The result was an uneasy policy of collaboration with the United Nations, at first loyal but laden with frustrations (1947–1958), then frankly hostile (1958–1965).

A reluctant collaboration (1947–1958)

UNTSO

From the start, France committed itself to behaving as a responsible permanent member. The first peace supervision intervention mounted by the United Nations found France ready to become involved in a foreign theatre of operations on behalf of the world Organization. In 1948, France participated actively in the discussion, preparation, and implementation of UNTSO, the United Nations Truce Supervision Organization. This first UN observation mission, which was to number as many as 500 observers in 1949, was, in a way, the first peace-keeping operation. The number of observers taken from the ranks of the French army to observe and maintain the cease-fire between Arabs and Israelis climbed from 21 to 125 between 1948 and 1949 (there were still 25 French officers in UNTSO from 1970 to 1980 and 18 in March 1996). Very early on, France paid its tribute to this first collective enterprise to establish peace. A French officer, Colonel Sérot, died when Count Folke Bernadotte, the United Nations mediator, was assassinated by Israeli extremists on 27 September 1948.

UNTSO had been launched under normal legal conditions (see chapter 2, below), respecting the predetermined equilibrium between the Security Council, the General Assembly, and the Secretary-General, even though the latter considerably enlarged the scope of his prerogatives at the time.

The Korean operation

The intervention in Korea, on the contrary, shattered the equilibrium provided for in the UN Charter and demonstrated the precarious nature of "great power" status conferred only by virtue of a permanent seat on the Security Council. The Security Council resolutions recommending, first, that members of the United Nations "furnish such assistance to the Republic of Korea as may be necessary to repel an armed attack and to restore international peace and security in the area,"[4] then, that they make all forces provided to assist the Republic of Korea "available to a unified command under the United States of America,"[5] were only possible, as is well known, because of the absence of the Soviet delegate. Once he had taken up his place on the Council again and used the veto power, the American Secretary of State, Dean Acheson, proposed that a resolution be adopted permitting the General Assembly to intervene in matters involving the maintenance of peace in any case where, due to a lack of unanimity between its permanent members, the Council was unable to carry out its responsibilities. France, together with the United Kingdom, nursed some doubts about the risks which might be implied by such an increase in the powers conferred on the General Assembly to the detriment of the Security Council. It attempted, in vain, to obtain a relaxing of the formulation of the resolution to require an affirmative vote of seven members of the Council for the convocation of the Assembly in emergency Special session, and a two-thirds majority vote for recommendations. On the substantial aspects, however, there was total capitulation.

By associating itself with Resolution 377 (V), adopted by the General Assembly on 3 November 1950, France accepted a major transformation in the functioning of the United Nations despite foreseeing that the Assembly might, one day, turn against it. At the time, however, France's main concern was to obtain international legitimacy in the combat against the Viet Minh in Indo-China. It needed the support of the Western world and, above all, American aid. More spectator than actor in an enterprise carried out entirely by the United States, France had little choice. A weak government (there were seven ministerial crises in France during the intervention in Korea), a budget in deficit, an increasing need for foreign aid, a tissue of errors and contradictions in an Indo-

China policy whose meanderings France's representatives at the United Nations had trouble following – all these problems hardly permitted an intransigent defence of the collective security system provided for in Chapter VII. France contributed to the operation in Korea along with 16 other nations: it sent an aviso, lent for a few months, an infantry battalion (3,000 soldiers) and medical supplies worth US$184,000. As long as the intervention lasted, France never ceased to compare the American action in Korea with its own action in Vietnam, affirming its solidarity "due to the action of the same nature" that it was under-taking in the region, whilst calling attention to the international character of the action undertaken "in the name of collective security."[6]

UNEF I

The Suez crisis of September-October 1956 marked a watershed in the history of peace-keeping. It was the occasion for the creation of the first United Nations Emergency Force (UNEF I), made up of "Blue Helmets" and without the participation of the great powers, a departure from the Charter which would come to be known as "Chapter VI-and-a-half." Already, all the elements of the controversy over the conduct of peace-keeping operations which would set France in opposition to the UN for many years were in place.

In political terms, the Franco-British expedition, led in response to the nationalization of the Suez canal by Egypt, was a total fiasco. At the United Nations, in a curious turn of events, the USSR, against which the Acheson Reso-lution had been conceived, voted with the United States to call an emergency Special session of the General Assembly. The aim was to get around the double veto, by France and the United Kingdom, of two resolutions calling for an immediate cease-fire (30 October 1956). France and the United Kingdom, which had earlier voted in favour of the Acheson Resolution, now attempted to oppose the transfer of the question to the General Assembly. Some days later, it became apparent that the proposed deployment of an international emergency force along the canal to ensure and survey the cessation of hostilities was the only honour-able way out. The British will had flagged and the attempt to pass off the inter-vention as a reprisal against aggression had failed. The United Nations offered the least disastrous means of disengagement possible, once the United States had condemned the expedition: it "wasn't glorious, but at least it was reasonable," the then Minister for Foreign Affairs, Christian Pineau, later confided.[7] France and the United Kingdom were forced to accept taking no part in UNEF nor having any recognized international mission for their troops, and to pull out without having obtained any global resolution of the management of the canal. The humiliation was immense and led to lasting resentment in France. The fact that Secretary-General Dag Hammarskjöld had skilfully avoided the dishonour of an explicit condemnation of the paratroop attack on Port Said passed totally unnoticed. A wave of furious nationalism turned public opinion against first the United States and then the United Nations. For having been the forum for the expression of general (and unexpected) disapproval of French policy, the United Nations was made the scapegoat.

Its back to the wall, France, as a permanent member of the Security Council, accepted the mounting of an operation not foreseen in the Charter and conceived by the General Assembly in a matter which involved it directly. The resolution of 4 November 1956 requesting the Secretary-General to submit a plan for the creation of UNEF I went unopposed. On 7 November, France voted in favour of the resolution laying down operational principles conceived by the Secretary-General. Moreover, in December, contrary to the United Kingdom and the USSR, France voted in favour of the resolution, inspired by the Secretary-General, to the effect that the expenses of deployment of UNEF I should be "apportioned among the Member States ... in accordance with the scale of assessments adopted by the General Assembly for contributions to the annual budget."[8] The implications of such a resolution were weighty as the permanent members of the Security Council had not only lost control of this type of operation but now found themselves obliged to provide the finance!

Torn between its immediate preoccupations and the desire to prepare for the future, incapable of choosing between its desire to manage colonial affairs in its own manner and its concern not to displease the United States, the France of the 1950s was on the defensive. Its policy in Morocco and Tunisia was regularly denounced by the United Nations. The Algerian cause was overtly supported by the General Assembly (although France was never formally "condemned" in a resolution). This displeased France but did not lead to any open crisis with the United Nations. France allowed the Secretary-General to take ever greater importance in peace-keeping matters and to conduct his own personal preventive diplomacy, including incessant travelling, sending representatives to conflict zones, and forming consultative committees on his own initiative, as in the Lebanese question in 1958 or Laos in 1959.

Conflicting relations (1958 – 1965)

The crisis broke with General de Gaulle's return to power in 1958. It first took the form of a personal confrontation between the General and the UN Secretary-General, who both had personalities out of the ordinary and were inspired in both cases by a quasi-mystical vision of history and of their own personal destinies. Against Dag Hammarskjöld, who had constructed a genuine doctrine of peace-keeping, UN intervention, and the role of the Secretary-General therein, General de Gaulle raised State sovereignty, the primary responsibility of the great powers for the maintenance of peace, and the fearless character of a France in control of its own choices. The UN intervention in the former Belgian Congo gave France the opportunity to show its disapproval of what constituted in its opinion a wrong turn for peace-keeping operations conducted by a public servant, albeit the Secretary-General of the United Nations with support from the General Assembly.

ONUC

At first (July 1960), France did not declare any principled opposition to the sending of a UN force to restore public order in the Congo, which took shape as "ONUC" (the more commonly used French acronym for UNOC), the United Nations Operation in the Congo. It would have preferred that the question be dealt with outside the United Nations by the major Western countries, but the weak response from Washington and the rapidity with which Dag Hammarskjöld greeted the request for assistance made by the new State caught France off guard. Its position was ambiguous. On one hand, it did not want to impede an action approved by Belgium, the underlying aim of which was to stop the USSR from gaining a foothold on the African continent. On the other hand, it was worried about creating a precedent justifying UN (and US) intervention in the internal affairs of a State when France itself was in the throes of war in Algeria. The failure of the operation would justify France's reluctance regarding this sort of operation, but the situation on the African continent, where France hoped to preserve its responsibilities, would be gravely complicated thereby. A UN success would increase the Secretary-General's influence a little more and encourage advocates of an Algerian solution within the framework of the United Nations.

As the situation in the former Belgian Congo deteriorated, leading Dag Hammarskjöld to interpret his mandate for the operation more and more widely, France toughened its position and disclosed its doubts on the appropriateness of "seeing an international organization substitute itself for national authorities in the exercise of their fundamental prerogatives and responsibilities."[9] The first Soviet veto in the case led to the convocation of an emergency Special session of the General Assembly on the basis of the Acheson Resolution (17 September 1960). France chose to abstain without explaining its vote. From that time on, the French delegation was instructed to abstain on all related resolutions and France declined "any participation in the operation in progress." It refused all access to French aerodromes (and those under its control in Africa) to UN aircraft and disapproved of any extension of the Secretary-General's mandate, whether it be Dag Hammarskjöld or his successor, U Thant. France refused to back the offensives led by ONUC to crush the Katanga secession late in 1961, and again in 1962. Moreover, as early as March 1961, France announced that it would not make any financial contribution towards the operation. To mark clearly the extent to which the United Nations was violating its own Charter by carrying on regardless of the Security Council blockage, France never used its veto power in the Congo crisis. Rather, it employed what Maurice Couve de Murville, then Minister of Foreign Affairs, described as its "only means" of action "or rather of reaction,"[10] the refusal to pay a financial contribution requested "illegally" by the General Assembly when it was up to the Security Council to command the operation and establish its cost.

Until the beginning of the 1970s, France stood by its position firmly and chose to abstain on any resolution authorizing the Secretary-General to undertake tasks outwith Security Council control. Thus, when U Thant managed to obtain the transfer of the Netherlands' administration of West Irian to a "United Nations Temporary Executive Authority" (UNTEA) in agreement with Indonesia, then requested General Assembly endorsement after the event, the vote in favour would have been unanimous if France had not abstained, taking all the French-speaking African nations with it (results: 89 for, 0 against and 14 abstentions).[11]

Even more significantly, when in March 1964 the Security Council was apprised of a resolution providing for the dispatch of an international peace-keeping force to Cyprus (UNFICYP) – a resolution prepared at great length by the Secretary-General, wished for by the United Kingdom, accepted by Greece, Turkey, and the government of Cyprus – France chose to abstain, along with the Soviet Union and Czechoslovakia, on the paragraph of the draft referring to the Secretary-General's mandate. It explained its vote by remarking that the Security Council was delegating particularly onerous duties to the Secretary-General, thereby offloading its own responsibilities (4 March 1964).

On the other hand, in 1965, when U Thant proposed a plan to the Security Council aimed at reinforcing the United Nations Military Observer Group in India and Pakistan (UNMOGIP), which had been deployed in the Kashmir region since 1949, France had no difficulty in voting in favour of the project because it had been thoroughly discussed by the members of the Council (4 and 6 September 1965). When, however, the Secretary-General took it upon himself to double UNMOGIP with another, entirely new force, the United Nations India Pakistan Observatory Mission (UNIPOM), merely informing the Council, the USSR protested against the illegality of the initiative and France remarked dryly that "if the Secretary-General always took care to ask the Council for instructions, he would avoid many difficulties" (25 October 1965).

Total reconciliation

A progressive improvement in relations

U Thant's prudence, however, won out over Dag Hammarskjöld's formidable ambitions for the United Nations. His position was rendered extremely vulnerable by the difficulties encountered in getting out of the Congo quagmire, the haughty vigilance of France and the Soviet Union, the financial crisis threatening to paralyse the Organization, and the imprecision of decisions concerning the creation, conduct, and financing of peace-keeping operations. U Thant was more aware of this fragility than his predecessors. For its part, France had found new confidence and stability. Its institutions were solid. The war in Algeria was finished. The decolonization in Africa had been a success, increasing France's prestige and its clientele at the United Nations. In this new climate, more confident relations grew up between the Secretary-General and French officials, especially as Mr Thant's position on American policy in Viet Nam was basically the same as that of General de Gaulle. These relations were barely troubled when, in 1967, U Thant was reproached for having pulled out UNEF I's contingents precipitately, simply at Egypt's request, without having consulted the Security Council. Then again, General de Gaulle would have preferred some dialogue among the Great Powers, any chance for which had been ruined by the Secretary-General's hasty action. Even so, France did not participate in the avalanche of criticism which was let loose on U Thant.

Another step was made towards total reconciliation between the French government and the UN system in October 1971 with the granting of a voluntary contribution to help the Organization out of its financial difficulties. While France did not reconsider its principled opposition regarding the financing of peace-keeping operations, nor its hostility towards special accounts, loans, and other financial facilities, it wanted to make a goodwill gesture.

In fact, the legal argument over peace-keeping operations had lost its *raison d'être*. The General Assembly now being dominated by African and Asian countries, the United States no longer had an automatic majority and none of the permanent members of the Security Council could be sure of getting a hearing. The Secretary-General was extremely prudent. The Security Council had regained its rights and has never lost them since. France prides itself on having buried the Acheson Resolution by taking away its automatic application in cases of Security Council blockage. Actually, on 7 February 1980, after days of intense consultations under French presidency, the Security Council decided to transfer the examination of the situation created by the deployment of Soviet troops in Afghanistan to the General Assembly without referring to Resolution 377 (V). Thirty years of precedent had been overturned! This new precedent was followed in January 1982.[12]

UNIFIL

The watershed in French policy towards peace-keeping was the deployment of a French contingent under the UN flag in Southern Lebanon in March 1978.

France's desire to play a role in the Middle East again, through participation in an international force sent to the region, was not new. After the Six-Day War, General de Gaulle had envisaged sending a peace force to replace UNEF I, which would have been decided through a quadripartite dialogue, outside the UN system, but he was not heeded. In 1973, when the composition of a new emergency force was discussed after the Arab-Israeli War, France asked to be included in UNEF II but the United States opposed it. In 1976, during a visit to the United States, Valéry Giscard d'Estaing had raised the possibility of sending French troops to Lebanon to separate the combatants if the Lebanese authorities requested it and all factions were in agreement. The negative reactions of the Arab world quashed any follow-up on the proposal. In March 1978, the invasion of Southern Lebanon by Israel swept away all hesitation. A French presence was wanted not only by the Lebanese authorities, due to strong cultural links and a long-held friendship, but also by the United States and the Secretary-General. The unwritten law which had excluded permanent members of the Security Council from peace-keeping operations until then (apart from special cases such as the British logistical support for UNFICYP from 1964 on) was put aside. On 19 March 1978, the decision to mount UNIFIL (the United Nations Interim Force in Lebanon) was taken in Paris and accepted in New York. Three days later, the first contingent of French paratroops arrived in Beirut; 1,380 soldiers would be deployed in all. For a long time, the French presence was the essential element of UNIFIL, by virtue of its numbers, permanence, and quality.

This first French participation in a peace-keeping force was a diplomatic success. The country's importance was recognized and its chances of participating in the establishment of a global regional settlement were improved. The force, however, was deployed in the worst of conditions, running major risks. In contrast to previous peace-keeping operations, now referred to as "the first generation," the deployment of UNIFIL did not come after an agreement between all the parties for the purpose of supervising and facilitating the cessation of hostilities. The mandate was vast and unrealistic. UNIFIL was supposed to intervene between the adversaries, persuade the Israeli forces to retreat, and restore Lebanese governmental authority in Southern Lebanon, all without the use of force.

Daily incidents, many of which cost the lives of Blue Helmets, and in the course of which the first commander of the French contingent was grievously wounded, illustrated, and still illustrate, the ambiguities of such a mission. All of the technical difficulties and contradictions encountered later in the former Yugoslavia by UNPROFOR were experienced by UNIFIL. In June 1982, the inability of UNIFIL to oppose the Israeli invasion sowed doubts about this sort of force. French diplomatic efforts to find a solution within the UN framework in June-July 1982 were rejected by the United States. Against the reinforcement of UNIFIL and the deployment of observers recommended by France, the

United States preferred sending a "multinational force" (MNF) comparable to that which had been deployed in the Sinai since April, mounted by countries belonging to the Western camp in order to sideline the USSR (France had a small participation). Two MNFs were thus deployed, France and Italy participating alongside the United States. The second MNF, called MNF II (Second Multinational Force in Beirut) disembarked in September 1982 and pulled out in March 1984. The French were the first to arrive and the last to leave. In between, MNF II suffered two appalling bomb attacks and lost 355 men – 262 Americans and 92 French.

Throughout 1983, France requested that a United Nations force be sent to replace MNF II, in which it was participating only so as to avoid the shame of being completely absent. Not only was France relegated to second position politically, because the negotiations between Lebanon and Israel were conducted outside the UN system under exclusive United States control (and France's attempts at providing its good offices between the Lebanese parties had not succeeded), but its men in the field were the victims of failures not of its own making.

The multiplication of incidents in 1985–1986, deliberate threats against UNIFIL, and a series of attacks on French Blue Helmets led France to consider withdrawing its troops. From spring 1986 on, France experienced its first "cohabitation" (the situation where the President and the Prime Minister represent different political tendencies), with a right-wing parliamentary majority and Prime Minister (Jacques Chirac) and a left-wing President (François Mitterrand). In a tone unheard for 25 years, the prime minister denounced the United Nations, saying, "Our soldiers are courageous and they obey an Organization which, alas, cannot shoulder its responsibilities."[13] In November 1986, the French contingent, which had been the most numerous until then, was reduced to 530 men. Since that time, France has participated in UNIFIL in proportions comparable to those of other contributing countries. Nevertheless, France has retained considerable weight in the operation due to the operational quality of its soldiers and the fact that it is the only country participating in UNIFIL which is a permanent member of the UN Security Council.

2 The present situation

The renewal of the Security Council, begun in 1987 with Gorbachev's "new thinking," reached its peak between 1990 (the Gulf crisis) and 1994 (successive failures in Somalia, Rwanda, and the former Yugoslavia). The flood of calls upon the United Nations placed the Organization in a novel situation. Peace-keeping operations multiplied, with varied fortunes. "Peace-keeping" operations commenced under Chapter VI were transformed into coercive operations under Chapter VII. Larger and larger forces were deployed under the UN flag in more and more diverse theatres of operations, with increasingly conflicting missions.

France's strong and active involvement

France has committed itself massively to this renewal. In mid-1993 it was the largest contributor of troops deployed under the UN flag, with more than 9,000 men. In 1995 it was still the third largest contributor in the world, after India and Pakistan. France is also one of the main financial contributors. The Secretary-General, Boutros Boutros-Ghali, found the most attentive ears and best support in Paris. Every government, whether left- or right-wing, has chosen to maintain close links between "the Blue Helmets and the tricoloured flag" with the justi-fication that "these close links are explained by France's political will. Refusing both isolationism and expansionism, it has, in effect, opted resolutely for an active world presence. The participation of French forces in the management of crises, at the service of peace, is a direct manifestation of this."[14]

In one way or another, France has participated in most of the peace-keeping operations set up between 1991 and 1995. By sending police and military police to El Salvador (ONUSAL, 1991), electoral monitoring observers to Haiti (UNMIH, 1994), mine disposal experts to Angola (UNAVEM III, 1995), France showed its deliberate will to put its confidence in these UN operations of a new kind, called "the second generation."[15]

The operations in Cambodia: UNAMIC, UNTAC

The resolution of the Cambodian conflict was the first sizeable French commit-ment in service of the United Nations since UNIFIL. As co-president of the Paris Peace Conference along with Indonesia, France had participated in the negotia-tions on Cambodia since the beginning, devoting much energy to them. It signed the Paris Peace Agreements on 23 October 1991 and made up part of the United Nations Advance Mission in Cambodia (UNAMIC), and its successor UNTAC (United Nations Transitional Authority in Cambodia, March 1992 to November

1993), the most extensive operation undertaken by the United Nations up until then. France contributed the second largest contingent, around 1,500 men. The French have made a lukewarm assessment of this large-scale operation, due as much to its political results as to the functioning of the United Nations. Proud as they were of their action in the field, the French troops came home extremely sceptical about the capacity of the United Nations to succeed in imposing peace in situations where peace does not exist.

The operations in Somalia: UNOSOM I, Restore Hope, UNOSOM II

While the operation in Cambodia turned out to be a half-success, the Somali operation was degenerating into a quagmire. France had taken active part in "Operation Restore Hope" with 2,000 men (9 December 1992 to 18 December 1993). This intervention should have marked the triumph of the very French notion of a "right of humanitarian intervention" and the new "grand design" of French foreign policy in the post-Cold War era. For the first time, indeed, the Security Council had authorized an emergency military operation with humanitarian aims, without the assent of the parties, under Chapter VII (S/Res/794, 3 December 1992). France committed itself with firmness: "France intends to be present, always under United Nations auspices, whenever the law must be respected or human lives preserved" (Pierre Beregovoy, then Prime Minister, 8 December 1992). On 9 December, the Armed Forces Chief of Staff, Admiral Jacques Lanxade, clearly laid down the alternatives: "either we use force or we pull out"; but he was referring to Bosnia ...[17]

Added to that of Cambodia, this experience of humanitarian aid and the attempted economic and administrative reconstruction of a country certainly contributed to enhancing the humanitarian dimension of the activities of the French army. The complete political failure of the United Nations in Somalia, however, put starkly into question the extent to which this involvement in humanitarian tasks is appropriate, and indeed the fundamental role of Blue Helmets.

The operations in former Yugoslavia: UNPROFOR

The United Nations' prevarication in the former Yugoslavia, and then the Organization's replacement by NATO in the search for and application of the peace process, only served to reinforce these doubts. In the European theatre, the United Nations have been pushed into the background, probably decisively. However admirable the work, courage, and devotion of the Blue Helmets may have been, the Organization lost credit with the local population. France will have to draw the lessons from the experience. It was the largest troop contributor in the former Yugoslavia (6,000 men deployed progressively from April 1992 on). It encountered both glory and humiliation. More than the others, it had its heroes and paid the price in blood: 56 dead and nearly 600 wounded.

From July 1991 to July 1995, the main objective of French diplomacy was to achieve some kind of "lull scenario" in the former Yugoslavia through law and diplomacy. There was no question of confronting the Serb army and militias by force. In the short term the aim was to obtain a cessation of hostilities and negotiate a political settlement regarding the borders, minority rights, and the relationship between the communities. The focus was on the deployment of peace-keeping forces to separate the belligerents and relieve the suffering of civilians and displaced persons while the negotiating process was going on. In the middle and long term, the purpose was to further a form of stability in this highly sensitive area that would prevent the conflict from spreading to the whole Balkan region and possibly the whole former Soviet empire. Meanwhile, European solidarity had to be retained notwithstanding the differences in analysis between France, Germany, and the United Kingdom. The UN peace-keeping presence in Bosnia was a substitute for assertive collective action, a lowest common denominator. For three years, this analysis led to a sort of "negative diplomacy":[18] the search for peace was a failure but the United Nations was helpful in preventing the fighting from spilling over and the dissension amongst the Western European countries from getting out of hand.

Following President Mitterrand's surprise visit in June 1992, testifying to a specific interest in Sarajevo fed by strong mobilization of public opinion, France deliberately adopted a policy of assuring humanitarian aid that could not be achieved without military support. It pushed for and supported the dozens of Security Council resolutions enlarging UNPROFOR's mandate and, from August 1992 on, authorizing the use of force in accordance with Chapter VII. In an attempt to end the agony of besieged Srebrenica, France proposed that the town be declared a "safe area" in April 1993. Five other towns were declared "safe areas" in May 1993. The United Nations committed itself to protecting the civilian population in these six predominantly Muslim Bosnian towns. We know what the results were.

A slight shift in the French stand on the role of the United Nations in the former Yugoslavia occurred in 1994, following the killing of a number of civilians in the Markale market in Sarajevo in February 1994. Throughout 1994, France advocated a tougher attitude towards the Serbs, pushing for a more "active mission" for the Blue Helmets and the clearer militarization of an operation started two years earlier as a simple interposition mission. The decision of the new French President, Jacques Chirac, to remove the evident ambiguities in French policy and deploy a rapid reaction force in Bosnia marked a turning point. The seizure of 300 Blue Helmets as hostages by the Serbs (May–June 1995) was the last straw. Enough was enough. France could not tolerate further humiliation. In June 1995, French policy was reversed. For the first time, the Serbs were clearly pointed out as those who were responsible for the attacks on the peace-keepers and humanitarian convoys and were to blame for the failure of the various peace plans. The rapid reaction force was intended to protect the people effectively and to impede any new aggression against the Blue Helmets, by force if needed. This move certainly facilitated a commitment by the United States, which had resisted too great an involvement in the crisis until then. It paved the way for a new process which would lead to the Dayton compromise some months later.

Politically, France's strong military presence allowed it to play a primary role at each stage of the conflict, to be in direct contact with influential countries (notably through the Contact Group created in April 1994 at its initiative), and to make itself heard in all the decision-making bodies.[19] The US recovery of the initiative at the end of summer 1995 laid bare the fragility of this leadership. To maintain its rank France must continue to pay the price. It is part of IFOR (the Implementation Force) leading a division of 12,000 men, of whom 7,500 are French, in the south-east on the Sarajevo – Mostar – Ploce axis, the most delicate part of the former Yugoslavia.

In Somalia, as in Cambodia and the former Yugoslavia, the Blue Helmets were confronted with ambiguous mandates which answered the needs of the situation in theory, but turned out in reality to be too ambitious given the means provided to carry them out. The French units were deployed in regions placed under their sole responsibility. They undertook military and humanitarian actions simultaneously, including security, control, and the reconstitution of embryonic local police forces as well as transporting humanitarian and medical aid, putting wells back in service, and other tasks. They also learned to cooperate with UN agencies and humanitarian NGOs, a new experience.

In search of a doctrine

France remains one of the major contributors to world peace, but it has lost ground in terms of doctrinal reflection on UN peace-keeping. It was one of the first countries to respond to Boutros Boutros-Ghali's *An Agenda for Peace*; the French memorandum proposed that Member States prepare rapid reaction forces composed of pre-identified units so as to make up an ensemble of "force units" at the United Nations' disposal at all times. Since then, France has been out-distanced by Canada, which tabled a project at the United Nations in September 1995 aimed at improving the efficiency of the planning, financial administration, and implementation of peace-keeping operations.[20] This project contains more than 20 proposals providing for, notably, the formation of a "vanguard force" which would allow the United Nations to set up a multi-functional force of 5,000 military and civilian personnel capable of being deployed rapidly, under the authority of a permanent operational staff of 30 to 50 people, more in periods of crisis. These proposals were elaborated without reference to the five permanent members of the Security Council, which upset France a little, and it was slow to respond. The proposals are now being widely discussed. They have the support of the Nordic countries – the project is now known as the "Canadian–Nordic project" – and a number of States have already set up a "group of friends of rapid reaction" to advance them. The French response to the *Supplement to An Agenda for Peace*, delivered to the Secretary-General on 18 January 1996[21] and based on an orientation memorandum dated 6 March 1995 by the former Armed Forces Chief of Staff, Admiral Lanxade, and translated into diplomatic language by Foreign Affairs, does not elucidate the French opinion on all the proposals.[22]

The doctrinal reflection in which France is engaged is being carried out in a context of profound strategic upheaval. The new French President, Jacques Chirac, has undertaken a thoroughgoing overhaul of French defence. The missions of the armed forces are now organized around four basic operational functions:[23] *dissuasion*, maintained at sufficiency levels but at a reduced proportion of the total; *prevention*, a new priority; *protection*, which will place more emphasis on the concept of internal security; and *"projection,"* which has become "the main field for conventional capabilities" concentrating the greater part of the armed forces' capacity.

The concept of *"projection"* is at the heart of the reform. It expresses a new, more dynamic, defence posture. It takes account of the fact that the commitment of forces will essentially take place outside and far from French territory. There is no direct menace to France's borders. Its security and defence are played out in foreign theatres of operations, in Europe "and in the world" which call France to its "international responsibilities." This "projection" will rely upon professional armed forces capable of acting with greater availability and efficiency. The new mechanism is designed to allow collaboration with diverse partners – NATO, the Western European Union, the United Nations, and so on.

The current doctrinal effort aims at establishing the form of this collaboration within the UN framework, defining peace-keeping more precisely and proposing solutions corresponding to the Organization's intervention needs. At the time of writing (mid-1996), it is being carried out essentially within the Defence Ministry, with Foreign Affairs working on the documents submitted by the military only to put them in the appropriate diplomatic style.

The French memorandum in response to the *Supplement to An Agenda for Peace* makes three major points. First, it enlarges the Secretary-General's typology of operations related to international peace and security, which extends to preventive diplomacy and preventive deployment, peacemaking, peace-keeping, post-conflict peace-building and enforcement action. France wishes to complete this list "in order to reflect more accurately the nature of operations that are deployed before a conflict has ended and are intended to restore peace or moderate the conflict by methods that involve both securing the parties' consent and constraint." As opposed to the Secretary-General's relatively rigid definitions, France has substituted more supple definitions allowing a UN intervention in intermediate situations, of which Rwanda is an example.

Admiral Lanxade's memorandum clearly distinguishes three categories of operations:

(1) Interventions within the framework of the provisions of Chapter VI to keep the peace *with the consent of all the parties* after *cessation of hostilities*; i.e. "peace-keeping."

(2) Interventions based on Chapter VII to favour a return to peace in a country in a state of civil war, where the security of the civilian populations is

gravely threatened, but where *no aggressor has been designated*; i.e. "peace-restoration."

(3) Interventions based on Chapter VII to re-establish or impose peace by forceful opposition against a *well-identified aggressor*; i.e. "peace-imposition."

This typological exercise has the advantage of clearly bringing out the twin problems of the purpose of the operations and the military instructions concerning the use of force. The three types of operations do not meet the same needs and operational requirements. Rules of engagement can be specified for each of them. In this manner, soldiers would no longer be placed in the untenable position of being obliged to witness violence against local populations without being able to react.

The second major point in the memorandum is the emphasis placed on the notion of *impartiality*, as opposed to that of neutrality, and the importance given to the use of force. UN troops must be given the means of completing their mandate by imposing conditions that are not yet accepted by the belligerents, if necessary. This implies the possibility of putting aside the anaesthetic requirement of neutrality and taking sides against one party or another.

Finally, France puts forward a number of different propositions, on the one hand, to put into effect and perfect the system of stand-by units and set up rapid deployment units; and on the other, to strengthen the capacity of the UN Military Staff, including the improvement of planning and command structures.

The climate in which the French doctrine is being elaborated is visibly positive. The propositions go a long way and show France to be ready, in principle, to take the lead in the use of force under UN auspices, even in extremely complex situations. Even so, it is likely that in practice, the lessons of Somalia, Cambodia, the former Yugoslavia, and Rwanda will persuade it to be very prudent. The refusal to mount an operation in Burundi in 1995–1996 is the first illustration.

The United Nations' credibility has been shaken. The Organization is far from the euphoria of 1990–1992. The political benefits of a massive engagement under the UN flag are no longer a foregone conclusion. Moreover, French budget overruns due to peace-keeping operations have been calculated, running to US$350 million (1.75 billion francs) for 1992 and US$1.1 billion (5.5 billion francs) in 1993. This weighs heavily on the defence budget at a time when

France is engaged in a costly restructuring of the defence system in a context of budgetary restrictions. The armed forces are beginning to wonder about the "profit" to them from peace-keeping operations of which they pay all the financial, human, and psychological costs, whereas other departments, particularly Foreign Affairs, reap the benefits. There is a very good chance that the estimated financial cost of any new engagement examined will affect the political decision.

3 The decision-making process

Each peace-keeping operation generates its own specific decisional mechanism. The game varies with the region concerned, the timing, the nature of the operation, and the importance of the issues to French interests. The decision is never simple. The process of choosing between several options implies conflicting influences, negotiations, and bargaining within the national system. The players are not always the same. Their relative weights in the diverse stages of decision-making are not predetermined. Their influence on the "decision-maker" or "decision-makers" is variable. Moreover, the decision is rarely a clearly identifiable decision made at a clearly identifiable moment. It is generally predetermined by a number of earlier decisions which have reduced the range of foreseeable solutions and the framework in which the choice will be made. Once made, the decision applies over a period of time and requires any number of minor decisions to be put into effect. Above all, the application of a decision implying participation in a multilateral action will be spread out over a long period of time, with all the attendant risks, such as the loss of the initial sense of the action undertaken, the difference between original ambitions and subsequent means, and the progressive reversal of ends and means, the latter sometimes supplanting the former. Only a detailed study of the positions taken at each stage of a peace-keeping operation could show the complexity of the decision-making process. Here we will merely set out a number of permanent features.

UN initiation

The special nature of decisions involving multilateral action should not be forgotten. As regards peace-keeping operations, consultations between operating partners take up much time during the preparatory phase, at multiple levels and in various places.

Within the Security Council, the practice of holding informal consultations between the three "Western" permanent members of the Security Council has grown to such an extent that a new acronym, "P3," has appeared, referring to the Permanent Three: the United States, the United Kingdom and France. The impetus comes from one of the States (often the US State Department), which submits a draft project as a basis for discussions. These exchanges then lead to quadripartite meetings including Russia. Finally, the five permanent members of the Security Council (P5) meet informally. This admittedly very aristocratic mode of operating has the benefit of accelerating the preparation of resolutions and creating a sense of community between the permanent representatives of the five Great Powers. Each representative is subject to government direction, keeping it informed and receiving instructions periodically. In this way, multilateral sensitivity continually finds its way back to national administrations.

Numerous bilateral contacts accompany decisions concerning peace-keeping operations. France has a privileged relationship with the United Kingdom, a permanent member of the Security Council and an important troop contributor, but also with the other NATO members and with its partners in the European Union. For the latter, in fact, this is a legal obligation. The Maastricht Treaty provides that:

> Member States which are also members of the United Nations Security Council will concert and keep the other Member States fully informed. Member States which are permanent members of the Security Council will, in the execution of their functions, ensure the defence of the positions and the interests of the union, without prejudice to their responsibilities under the provisions of the United Nations Charter. (Art. J. 5.)

This provision has led to slight changes in the way in which France perceives its Security Council membership. Until the end of the 1980s, there was no question of admitting officially that France "concerted" with its EU partners. Even "information" was hardly referred to, as it appeared essential that France make declarations to the Security Council in its own name without representing any other country, so as to counter any possible proposal for a reform creating a common rotating seat for member countries of the then European Community. Since then, France can use Europe to increase its power, using one of its trump cards, its pivotal role in European construction and the ability to draw the rest of the European countries in the wake of the Franco-German couple. France retains,

however, the right to choose. The formula, "without prejudice to their responsibilities under the provisions of the United Nations Charter," added to the
Maastricht Treaty at France's request, allows for wide interpretation. Until
now, France has transmitted all of its observations on peace-keeping to the UN
Secretary-General on its own behalf, in the name of its specific responsibilities.

The role of the national institutional powers

The executive power

Since 1958, the provisions of the Constitution and their interpretation have led to
an extreme personalization of the conduct of French foreign and military policy.
The President of the French Republic, Head of State, holds powers unequalled
in other grand democracies. Elected for seven years and not responsible before
Parliament, he is the guarantor of national independence, the integrity of the
territory and the respect of treaties (Art. 5), negotiates and ratifies treaties (Art.
52) and is the sole representative of France in "summits." The President is the
Commander-in-Chief of the Armed Forces and chairs higher national defence
councils and committees (Art. 15); he alone can fire strategic nuclear weapons.[24]
The President defines the major lines of foreign and defence policy and no
important initiative may be taken without his decision. He can personally
authorize a rapid military intervention without convening a defence council
or consulting Parliament. When the presidential majority coincides with that of
Parliament, which is ordinarily the case, the President of the Republic is the
incontestable and uncontested master of foreign and military policy.

The role of the Prime Minister, Head of Government, is normally more one of
execution than of creating impetus. He or she takes action to give effect to decisions made at the Elysée Palace, the official residence of the French President,
and yet the Constitution gives the Prime Minister important powers. The government determines and conducts national policy (which clearly includes foreign
policy) and the armed forces are "at its disposal" (Art. 20). The Prime Minister
directs the conduct of government affairs and is responsible for national defence
(Art. 21). During periods of "cohabitation" these provisions of the Constitution
take on their full importance. (There have been two such periods, 1986–1988

and 1993–1994, since the beginning of the fifth Republic in 1958.) A more or less conflictual diarchy originates between the incumbent at the Elysée Palace and that of the Hôtel Matignon, the offices of the French Prime Minister. Foreign policy remains personalized, but with two "decision-makers" at the top.

The bureaucracy

However important the President (and sometimes the Prime Minister) may be, no head of state or government decides everything, all alone. The "decision-maker" surrounds himself or herself with counsellors and helpers and depends on the services of the Administration. In the management of matters dealt with by the UN Security Council, the French Minister of Foreign Affairs plays an essential role. The political impetus is given by the Elysée (or, very rarely, by Matignon) but the instructions destined for the French permanent representative on the Security Council are given by the political affairs department of the "Quai d'Orsay," the offices of the French Department of Foreign Affairs, and more particularly, by its United Nations and International Organizations Bureau. This service has a staff of around 40, of whom 20 are drafters, specialized by geographic area, who normally prepare draft instructions on questions raised in the Security Council. Very often, in fact, these instructions result from information received from the permanent mission in New York. The post of Ambassador, the permanent representative of France on the Security Council, is most prestigious. Its incumbents are always listened to, if not always understood. As regards peace-keeping operations, the elaboration of instructions requires quasi-permanent inter-ministerial consultations. Apart from the Foreign Ministry's Political Department, the relevant Geographical Department and quite often the Legal Department, a number of other ministries are concerned, including in all cases the Ministry of Defence, and sometimes the Ministries of Transport (in cases of embargo), Justice (when actions before an international tribunal or the dispatching of French judges are involved), or the Interior (when policemen are deployed or local government employees sent to observe elections), and, of course, the Ministry of Finance.

This practice of inter-ministerial consultation, especially the daily contacts between the departments of Foreign Affairs and Defence, allow a rapid reaction to the extremely varied requests which can come from the UN Secretariat in response to Security Council resolutions. If the political line defined by the Elysée and transmitted by the cabinet of the Minister of Foreign Affairs is clear, the administrative machine is capable of responding promptly. France now has some know-how in peace-keeping matters. "In most cases we are able to respond to a request for logistic support, rotation of military aircraft or deployment of police and military police, within 24 hours, where certain of our partners take some days, or even weeks."[25]

When the decision involves the deployment of a large-scale armed force, the collaboration between civil and military staff takes place at the highest level.[26] The Head of State remains master of the aims and judge of the means. Plans proposed to him are prepared under the responsibility of the Armed Forces Chief of Staff, in collaboration with the President's personal Chief of Staff and in close contact with the Defence Minister and the General Secretary to the Presidency. The progress of operations is followed at all times by the Armed Forces Staff, the President's civil and military cabinet, and the Defence Minister.

It sometimes happens that a restricted council is set up to meet weekly so as to maintain collaboration and avoid discord on a particularly difficult and politically sensitive matter. The Prime Minister, the Armed Forces Chief of Staff, the President's personal Chief of Staff, the General Secretary to the Presidency, and the Minister of Foreign Affairs all participate. Such a council was set up by François Mitterrand in February 1993, for example, to deal with matters related to the former Yugoslavia. During the second "co-habitation" this meeting tended to be "one of the most important points of contact between the President and the government for crisis management."[27]

This exemplary collaboration between civilian authorities and military leaders in the conduct of peace-keeping operations, and the uncontested supremacy of civilian power in the decision-making process, cannot hide the reservations of the military hierarchy inspired by the multiplication of foreign interventions for which neither the mission, the command structure, nor the means are clearly defined. The play on words made by a high-ranking military officer, referring to UNPROFOR, and repeated continuously in the spring of 1995 – "either we fire or we retire" ("on tire ou on se retire") – shows real impatience.[28]

The legislative power

A 1992 standing committee report on the Finance Bill written by François Trucy, a Senator from the Var *département*, criticized "the uncertainty and anxiety raised by the way in which these operations are conducted, sometimes placing our forces in such a difficult situation that their action in the field is all the more meritorious."[29] Amongst the uncertainties, he listed "costly operations and hypothetical finances" which allow neither operational necessities to be satisfied nor the basic requirements of force protection to be met. As for anxieties, he denounced "UN deficiencies" including badly adapted structures, a fluctuating and ill-defined political project, and, above all, the absence of clear rules of engagement. "French incoherence" was also deplored in terms recalling the French right wing's traditional complaints about the United Nations, including "Anglo-Saxon and Third World infiltration" of the Organization, and a weak French presence in the Secretariat which "deprives it of the chance of direct influence and, in the longer term, the means of changing and improving the working of the system." Having been written by a then opposition MP, the report contained elements of internal polemic. It was meant to serve as an argument for refusing to adopt the defence budget, a classic and rather inconsequential game as long as there is a stable parliamentary majority. Even so, in the end, the findings of the report were never refuted. Widely diffused and commented on in the press, they are indicative of a real uneasiness at the highest levels of the defence forces.

Soon afterwards, the Prime Minister commissioned a study of French participation in peace-keeping operations from the same MP. The aim was to study the extent to which the means placed at the disposal of the United Nations by France were adapted to its missions, specifically with respect to the preparation of the forces and their equipment, the organization of troop rotations, the integration of forces within the UN system in different theatres of operations, and the living and working conditions of the forces in the field. Also to be analysed was the financing of such operations and the national defence budget cost overruns resulting from participation in them. Senator Trucy's voluminous report gathers together a large amount of information on all these questions and suggests specific responses. The senator puts forward concrete propositions, many of which, especially those concerning structural and procedural reform of the UN, have been transformed into official requests by France to the UN Secretariat.

The Trucy report's conclusions are clear. It answers in the affirmative the three questions: must France participate in peace-keeping operations? does it know how to do so? is it capable of doing so?

To defend our country's interests well, France must be strong, present wherever that presence is necessary, accepted, recognized, and if possible solicited by the international community.

By the interests of France I mean diplomacy, influence, culture, economic markets, commerce, industry, services ...

The French, whether they be military or civilian, professionals or NGOs, have demonstrated their capacity to accomplish most of the tasks required by UN resolutions, despite any unforeseen difficulties – at least, all those which were feasible, given the serious imperfections in the UN system.

The French Armed Forces have adapted rapidly to the style and requirements of these new operations. Yes, France has the know-how.

But there are conditions:

If no tangible significant and consequential sign of progress in UN management of PKOs were to be noted soon, it would be up to France to draw the conclusions concerning the size of its present and future contributions to PKOs and with regard to the security of our troops as well as our fundamental defence interests.[30]

This report reflects widespread opinion, especially in defence circles.

Standing committee reports aid in the formation and expression of public opinion. They also add to doctrinal reflection, but politically, Parliament's role in the definition of French policy concerning peace-keeping is non-existent. Representatives do not take part in the decision to commit forces to foreign theatres of operations. Article 35 of the Constitution, according to which "declarations of War shall be authorized by Parliament," does not apply to peace-keeping operations because no war is declared. This is so even for operations launched in accordance with Chapter VII. During the Gulf War, Parliament was convened for an extraordinary session. The government tabled a motion of confidence in the National Assembly (the lower House of Parliament) and made a general policy declaration before the Senate, followed by a vote. This extra-ordinary session was, however, only convened because of the Executive's desire to "inform" and "associate" the Parliament and not to request its "authorization." The session was dismissed immediately after the vote. Just like other citizens, the representatives were later informed of the decision during a broadcast presidential address.

National representatives are generally kept out of decisions to commit French forces to peace-keeping operations, more because it has tended to relinquish its involvement than because of any lack of jurisdiction or of experts capable of giving food for thought. It is not uncommon for debates on foreign and defence policy to take place before an almost empty House, with the MPs finding better things to do elsewhere. Thus, on 7 June 1996, only 30 per cent of MPs participated in the vote on new military programming legislation, or 167 out of 576 representatives. Apart from a few rare exceptions, Parliament has given in as far as defence and foreign policy matters are concerned. At most, it plays the role of sounding board but exerts no real pressure.

The influence of other actors

Public opinion

The United Nations' failures in Somalia, and, even more, in former Yugoslavia, have raised many questions about the pertinence of the characteristics peculiar to missions entrusted to the Blue Helmets, notably the obligation of non-use of force, but no one in France, on the whole, criticizes the basic principle of national participation in peace-keeping operations. The French are even proud of it.

When French forces were first placed at the disposal of the United Nations in 1978, unrestrained press headlines reported "the French intervention in Lebanon" and "French forces in Lebanon." It took time and casualties, the wounded and the dead, to bring the understanding that the French forces were subject to a United Nations mandate and were not acting alone. Media coverage of peace-keeping operations in which French soldiers are participating is strong. Night after night, when the going gets tough in the field, the television news exalts the bravery and exemplary behaviour of the French Blue Helmets and their attention to the local population. It is true that the Armed Forces Information and Public Relations Service (SIRPA), which showed some failings during the Gulf War, has become very professional. The question of relations with the press is taken very seriously into account by military leaders in Paris and in the field. In the theatre of operations, the management of relations with the local media has become an integral part of the mission. This was true in former Yugoslavia and even more so in Rwanda. In Paris, communications are aimed at the families of the Blue Helmets and the general public, upon whom national morale depends (i.e. the degree of popular support for the operation decided upon by the political powers and the extent to which it can accept sacrifice and death).

SIRPA regularly polls French opinion of foreign interventions. This has remained relatively stable despite hostage-taking and the loss of many soldiers during peace-keeping operations. When asked if they approve or disapprove of the use of French armed forces, the French have replied as follows:[31]

"Within the framework of the United Nations for the respect of international law": 81 per cent would have approved in June 1995, 82 per cent in 1991, and 84 per cent in 1992, 1993, and 1994. The heavy toll paid for peace-keeping operations seems to have reduced general approval only a little.

"To bring assistance to populations in distress (famine and civil war)": 78 per cent would have approved in June 1995, 73 per cent in 1990, 79 per cent in 1991, 81 per cent in 1992 and 1993, and 83 per cent in 1994.

"To contribute to the re-establishment of peace in a region of the world": 58 per cent approved in May 1988, before the end of the Cold War, 27 per cent disapproved, and 15 per cent had no opinion. During the Gulf War, in May 1991, 70 per cent approved and 20 per cent disapproved, 10 per cent having no opinion. In June 1995, 73 per cent approved, 20 per cent disapproved and 7 per cent had no opinion. At the same time, while 200 Blue Helmets were being held hostage by the Serbs and the debate was intensifying in France over the appropriateness of maintaining UNPROFOR, 91 per cent of people polled declared their approval of the use of French armed forces *"to obtain the liberation of French hostages"*; 6 per cent were against and 5 per cent had no opinion. A large majority also appeared to approve foreign interventions aimed at *"destroying a terrorist centre (e.g. a training camp)"*: 84 per cent approved, 11 per cent were against, and 5 per cent were of no opinion.

This general approval of France's engagement in favour of international security must be qualified when specific operations are mentioned. On 10 August 1992, when Sarajevo was being bombarded day and night and the Security Council was examining the possibility of acting under Chapter VII, 61 per cent of the French polled said they were in favour of *"French participation in a military intervention in Bosnia and Herzegovina within the UN framework"*; 33 per cent were against, and 9 per cent had no opinion.[32] Even so, optimism about UN effectiveness is weak. When asked, *"Do you think a real United Nations armed intervention would bring the war to an end or, on the contrary, lead to a worsening of the conflict?"*, only 48 per cent of those polled considered that it would put an end to the war; 33 per cent thought it would worsen the conflict, with 19 per cent expressing no opinion.[33]

The French are reluctant to envisage military interventions which might put French Blue Helmets at risk. On 9 January 1994,[34] 51 per cent declared themselves to be against *"brutal military action, aerial attacks for example, knowing the risks they create for our soldiers on the ground"*; only 44 per cent were in favour. A closer analysis reveals extremely divided opinions: 30 per cent "fairly favourable," 31 per cent "fairly unfavourable." A later poll, taken on 18 February 1994 just before the expiration of the NATO ultimatum to the Serbs, gave much the same results. In response to the question *"Are you completely in favour, fairly in favour, fairly opposed or completely opposed to French participation in ground operations in the former Yugoslavia?"*, 53 per cent were in favour and 43 per cent opposed (18 per cent completely in favour, 19 per cent completely opposed, 35 per cent fairly in favour, and 24 per cent fairly opposed). With public opinion in such a perplexed state, the slightest incident could swing opinions from moderate support to massive refusal.

In any case, the answer to one question was clear. Even before the operation got to the point of military intervention, 68 per cent of the French polled declared that it would be *"unacceptable for France to lose a considerable number of soldiers in the former Yugoslavia"*; only 29 per cent considering that *"the idea that France may lose a considerable number of soldiers in the former Yugoslavia must be accepted."*

Media and "humanitarians"

The formation of French public arises in an unusual context which unites the media, the political class, and a few professional heralds of humanitarian causes.

The link between the audio-visual press and political power is an old one. It is less restrictive than during the de Gaulle era, but remains strong. Television stars, major leader-writers, and politicians make up a "Parisian microcosm" who know each other, meet in the same places, and share the same codes. This results in a certain connivance and a form of self-censorship unparalleled in the Anglo-American press. This does not mean that the press is under orders or that it hushes up all criticism, but it does mean that holders of political power have the means to use it to convey their messages and send signals. In this way the government contributes to a major extent to the formation of public opinion.

The connivance between the media, politics, and humanitarianism began in the 1970s with the creation of the non-governmental organization, *Médecins sans Frontières*, by Bernard Kouchner, Claude Malhuret, and Rony Brauman, followed by *Médecins du Monde*, created by Kouchner alone. Many of those who were to give a world-wide reputation to French humanitarian assistance – the "French doctors" – were also remarkable debaters, just as gifted at forcing their way onto television as onto the political scene. Thus it was that Claude Malhuret became the first Secretary of State for Human Rights of a right-wing government (during the first "cohabitation" of 1986–1988) while Bernard Kouchner was named Secretary of State for Humanitarian Action, then Minister of Public Health and Humanitarian Action, once the Left regained power (1988–1993). Under the influence of "without borderism" a sheer "humanitarian ideology" began to spread in France, infiltrating editorial offices, government administration, schools, and all sectors of public opinion. One of the most resounding examples was the proclamation in 1987 of the "right to humanitarian assistance and the obligation of States to contribute to it" at a large conference gathering together all of "committed" Paris, opened by François Mitterrand and concluded by Jacques Chirac. As Alain Pellet comments, *"Justified by studies, often of great quality, prepared by the directors of humanitarian NGOs or lawyers, backed by the highest state authorities, accompanied by a large-scale media build-up, this declaration partially renewed the traditional debate on interventions of humanity, rebaptized for the occasion as the duty to intervene (devoir d'ingérence)."*

Discussion of the "right" or "duty" to intervene for humanitarian reasons has fuelled a very mediatized Franco-French debate for a number of years. Under the influence of Bernard Kouchner and his collaborators (especially the jurist Mario Bettati), it permeated French diplomacy between 1987 and 1994. The debate built up a very strong sentiment of moral obligation in public opinion that there is a duty, if not a *right*, to bring assistance to victims of famine, war, and catastrophes of all kinds throughout the world. The climate was thus favourable for the unprecedented linking of military and humanitarian action seen since Resolution 688 (1991), continuing up to Operation Turquoise in Rwanda (1994). The political leaders wanted it. Humanitarian groups were pushing for it. Public opinion was ready for it. Nevertheless, it would be wrong to think of private humanitarian organizations as playing a decisive part in political decision-making in France. They created the climate. They renewed debate. They often brought pressure to bear. They have undoubtedly contributed to making humanitarian action a supplementary dimension of foreign policy. Their processes have influenced, and still influence, official thinking on the concepts of neutrality and impartiality. Notwithstanding all this, forceful intervention for humanitarian motives is always decided upon for a complex array of reasons in which NGO pressure is but one element amongst others, sometimes decisive, sometimes not.

First of all, private humanitarian organizations are rarely in agreement amongst themselves. Not all have the same doctrinal position and their rivalry covers whole columns of the French newspapers. Many are extremely hostile to the amalgamation of separate issues and to the incursion of the military into humanitarian affairs. In addition, political pressure brought to bear through the media does not come from highly structured organizations capable of action comparable, for example, to that of CARE in the United States for the intervention in Somalia. It comes from a small number of key figures with access to the public: intellectuals, artists, journalists, and political orators. Thus, the strong mobilization of French public opinion concerning the siege of Sarajevo, and the calls for the United Nations to destroy the Serb sniper force dug in on the surrounding mountains, came more from intellectuals indignant at the reappearance of concentration camps and ethnic cleansing "two hours from Paris" than from humanitarian NGOs. Finally, the game goes both ways. Politicians use the humanitarian ideology at least as much as they are subjected to it. When Operation Turquoise in Rwanda was being organized by the Elysée and the Quai d'Orsay for complicated reasons of African policy, the first question those concerned asked themselves was how to make it acceptable to public opinion and which medium to choose so as to avoid the appearance of a neo-colonial expedition.[36] The existence of a climate favourable to humanitarian intervention was quite convenient.

Notes

1. The "Territories" (*territoires*) are quasi-self-governing units, whereas the "Departments" (*départements*) are considered to be administrative sub-units of the French State.

2. F. Trucy, "Participation de la France aux opérations de maintien de la paix," p. 69.
3. See Alfred Grosser, *La IVe République et sa politique extérieure* [The foreign policy of the Fourth Republic], Paris: Armand Colin, 1967.
4. S/Res/83, 27 June 1950.
5. S/Res/84, 7 July 1950.
6. Jean Chauvel, S/PV.474th meeting, 27 June 1950.
7. Christian Pineau, *1956 – Suez* (Paris: Laffont, 1976) p. 206.
8. A/Res/1089, 21 December 1956.
9. UN Security Council, 15 September 1960.
10. Maurice Couve de Murville, *Une politique étrangère, 1956–1969* [A foreign policy, 1956–1969] (Paris: Plon, 1971), p. 459.
11. A/Res/1752 (XVII), 21 September 1962.
12. Jacques Leprette, "Le Conseil de sécurité et la résolution 377/V" [The Security Council and Resolution 377 (V)], *Annuaire français de droit international*, 1988, pp. 424–35.
13. *Le Monde*, 28 August 1986.
14. François Léotard, Defence Minister, in André Lewin (ed.), *La France et l'ONU depuis 1945* [France and the UN since 1945] (Paris: Arléa-Corlet, 1995), p. 193.
15. Georges Abi-Saab, "La deuxième génération des opérations de maintien de la paix" [The second generation of peace-keeping operations], *Le Trimestre du Monde* 4, 1992, pp. 87–97.
16. See the revelations of General Loridon, former head of the military wing of UNAMIC and deputy head of UNTAC, in Fondation pour les études de défense (FED), *Opérations des Nations Unies: leçons de terrain, Cambodge, Somalie, Rwanda, ex-Yougoslavie* [United Nations operations: lessons from the field, Cambodia, Somalia, Rwanda, former Yugoslavia], Paris: La Documentation française, 1995.
17. See Maurice Torelli, "Les missions humanitaires de l'armée française" [The French army's humanitarian missions], *Revue de défense nationale*, March 1993; pp. 65–78; Philippe Guillot, "France, peacekeeping and humanitarian intervention," *International Peacekeeping*, Spring 1994, pp. 30–43.
18. Patrice Canivez, "La France ambigüe: des paroles et des actes" [France's ambiguity: words and deeds], in Jean Cot (ed.), *Dernière guerre balkanique? Ex-Yougoslavie: témoignages, perspectives* [The last Balkan war? Former Yugoslavia: personal accounts and perspectives] (Paris: Harmattan/FED, 1996), p. 196.
19. See Alex Macleod, "La France: à la recherche du leadership international" [France: in search of international leadership], *Relations internationales et stratégiques* 19, Autumn 1995, pp. 69–80.
20. Canadian Government (Foreign Affairs and National Defence Ministries), *United Nations Peacekeeping Operations: Toward a Rapid Reaction Capability for the United Nations*, September 1995.

21. S/1996/71, 30 January 1996.
22. His letter, entitled "Orientations pour la conception, la préparation, la planification, le commandement et l'emploi des forces françaises dans les opérations militaires fondées sur une résolution du Conseil de sécurité des Nations Unies" [Guidelines for the conception, preparation, planning, command, and deployment of French forces in military operations based on Resolutions of the UN Security Council], was published in *Objectif 21, Revue du commandement, de la doctrine et de l'entraînement*, 1995/1, "La doctrine militaire française pour les opérations de maintien de la paix" [French military doctrine for peace-keeping operations].
23. Speech by Jacques Chirac at the Military School, Paris, 23 February 1996.
24. On all these points see Samy Cohen, *La monarchie nucléaire* [The nuclear monarchy], Paris: Hachette, 1986.
25. Gabriel Keller (former vice-director for the United Nations and International Organizations at the "Quai d'Orsay"), "La France et le Conseil de sécurité" [France and the Security Council], *Le Trimestre du Monde* 4, 1992, p. 43.
26. On the relations between civil and military questions, see Samy Cohen, *La défaite des généraux* [The defeat of the generals] (Paris: Fayard, 1994), especially pp. 124–35.
27. Cohen, *La défaite des généraux*, p. 135.
28. This anxiety is not limited to the military. Cf. FED, *Opérations des Nations Unies; leçons de terrain*.
29. François Trucy, "Rapport général sur le projet de loi des finances," Sénat no. 56, T.III–An. 43, 24 November 1992.
30. F. Trucy, "Participation de la France aux opérations de maintien de la paix," p. 196.
31. Source: SIRPA: SOFRES.
32. IFOP poll.
33. SOFRES poll for France Television, taken on 7 and 8 January 1994.
34. BVA poll.
35. Alain Pellet, *Droit d'ingérence ou devoir d'assistance humanitaire?* [Right to intervene or duty of humanitarian assistance?] (Paris: La Documentation française, 1995), p. 5.
36. Account given to the author at the Ministry of Foreign Affairs.

2

LEGAL ASPECTS

Yves Daudet

If, from a political perspective, France's position with respect to the United Nations has varied with the diverse situations and constraints to which it has been subject,[1] seen from a legal perspective, its position has been characterized by marked continuity. At first sight this contrast may seem surprising. It is not so astonishing, however, given that, in order to face the evolving political situation over the last fifty years, the United Nations has had to improvise, finding innovative answers on the fringes of the Charter. France, on the other hand, has been guided by a relatively constant concern with respect for the Charter, generally remaining reserved regarding any bending of the rules deviating from the constitutional system and the spirit of the institutions set up in San Francisco.

This overall position should not be attributed to an exaggerated concern for legalism but simply to the fact that France, as a permanent member of the Security Council, considers the institutional balance (particularly the primary responsibility for peace-keeping matters conferred on the Security Council) to be the best means of protecting its own interests. For all that, there have been exceptions. For instance, France unenthusiastically rallied to the Acheson Resolution even though, at the time of its adoption, the resolution was supported by a pro-American majority in the General Assembly which did not necessarily serve French interests. Being a colonial power, France ran the risk of encountering more hostility than support from a General Assembly in which Third World representation was growing, as we have seen in the preceeding chapter. When the General Assembly ceased to be pro-American in the 1970s (and the United States first used its veto in the Security Council), the Assembly's non-alignment lent it an aura of unpredictability in contrast with the certainty offered by the veto power over Security Council action. All things considered, France has used the veto power sparingly (only 18 times). In fact, France simply counts on its presence, relying on this to assure quasi-automatic membership of the subsidiary organs within the United Nations.[2]

This is the means by which France intends to maintain its rank as a Great Power. The reality of this status matters little, in the end, in a world now composed of the United States first, followed by all the "other" States. From now on, for France, being just "another" State, the main thing is to make sure that it enjoys all the benefits of the status conferred on it in 1945. France's attachment to the principles and rules of the Charter comes fully within the scope of this logic and explains the legal orthodoxy it defends.

In this way, France's position towards the United Nations varies in line with the evolution of the Organization's approach to its own Charter. If at present, France is more present and active in the United Nations than ever, it is because the managerial role of the Security Council and that of the "P5" (or even the "P3"), within which French diplomacy is currently extremely active, has become so assertive since the end of the Gulf crisis as to be quasi-exclusive.

Thus it is that, through a return to the original institutional balance of the Charter, France is better able to make itself heard and assert itself. There is no doubt that, in today's uni-polarized context, France can play a role through the United Nations that it could not fulfil alone. In this way its essential policies are well served by application of the Charter and respect for the law of the United Nations.

I The constitutional framework

When we are speaking of France, constitutional aspects must be envisaged from a double perspective. In the first place, it is necessary to look into a question which has long been hotly debated, that of the constitutionality of peace-keeping operations with regard to the Charter. This problem has been of great importance to France, which, as we will show, has always been and still is strongly attached to respect for the Charter, to the extent of creating a crisis in relations between France and the United Nations.

Peace-keeping operations also raise numerous questions of constitutionality with regard to French domestic law, the second subject of analysis.

France and the constitutionality of peace-keeping operations with respect to the United Nations Charter

In 1945, the Charter created a subtle institutional balance between the General Assembly and the Security Council with a view to achieving the "goal of goals" of the United Nations, namely the maintenance of international peace and security. The importance of the issue at stake justified giving both principal organs the power to have such matters referred to them and to discuss them, but it also justified avoiding any rivalry in the conduct of peace-keeping actions which might end in contradiction. For these reasons a certain pre-eminence was given to the Security Council in this domain. Article 12 gives it priority over the General Assembly in the exercise of its peace-keeping functions, while Article 11, paragraph 2, gives it a monopoly over all "action." By blocking the principal active organ, the Cold War had a direct effect on this system and obliged the United Nations to invent new processes for the preservation of peace, on the basis that the goal to be attained transcended the constitutional rules set out in the Charter and that it was advisable to develop the means rendered necessary by the new political context of the Cold War and bi-polarity. No United Nations army ever having been set up, the *ersatz* "Blue Helmets" were invented. In the absence of one of the permanent members of the Security Council, it was decided, through an audacious reading of Article 27, paragraph 3, that an abstention was not equivalent to a veto. In the face of a blocked Security Council, the Acheson Resolution permitted the General Assembly to take over from the body in default. This is one example, among others, of the range of additions, improvisations, and teleological interpretations which have kept the system working while exposing its powerlessness. Whilst the French attitude, which was not particularly radical, was subject to a number of adjustments or exceptions, it was always marked by a certain reserve with regard to these practices, taking the form of fairly clear opposition and even going so far as the use of the financial weapon of refusing to contribute to certain expenditures related to peace-keeping on the basis that they were unconstitutional. This had the added effect of extending what was already, thirty years ago, a financial crisis in the United Nations.

At that time, the French position was marked by great firmness, including the refusal to accept the distinction, suggested by the "Committee of 33," between a "static" conception, based on the strict interpretation of treaties, and a so-called "dynamic" interpretation designed to adapt the United Nations to supposedly changing circumstances. This distinction was considered questionable by France, which saw in it a "value judgment based on questionable criteria, at the very least,"[3] whereas France simply considered the United Nations Charter to be a multilateral treaty incapable of being revised other than in accordance with the procedure "provided for by the Charter and accepted by all the signatories."[4] The Charter system was described as a "prudent balance."[5] The permanent representative of France felt that the balance sought in 1945 was still valid twenty years later to and that "the current crisis shows what happens when an attempt is made to get around one of the fundamental principles underpinning the Charter."[6]

It was during this crisis and in the light of the further details provided by the International Court of Justice in its Advisory Opinion of 20 July 1962[7] that France was led to set out its constitutional interpretation of the Charter system.

The French position at the time the first PKOs were set up: Respect for the balance between the Security Council and the General Assembly

An analysis of the distribution of powers between the General Assembly and the Security Council requires a definition of the word "action" appearing in Article 11, paragraph 2 of the Charter. Certain States have interpreted the powers of the Security Council restrictively by limiting them to the "coercive" action referred to in Chapter VII. The result would be that Article 11, paragraph 2 would address a number of other categories of non-coercive actions (à voir avec le traducteur) undertaken at the request or with the consent of the State in question, involving no use of weapons except in self defence or in operations aimed at maintaining internal order by interposition between parties or factions without involving action against another State. All such actions, coming under Chapter VI or even, in some cases, "Chapter VI-and-a-half,"[8] would thus fall within the powers of the General Assembly.

France rejects this interpretation categorically, especially the distinction between operations conducted against a State (the only coercive actions) and operations to maintain internal law and order. First, the permanent representative of France underlined the fact that internal conflicts can easily degenerate into international conflicts. Admittedly, the pertinence of this observation was largely borne out in the course of the following years, and it is even more relevant at present.[9] The permanent representative observed further that the fact that the government in question had given its consent to the presence of UN forces on its territory did not convert an international conflict into internal troubles. Third, he refused to accept that an "action" would not be coercive just because the authorization to use force was exceptional or given only in case of self-defence. In this respect, it is worth noting that the concept of self-defence can be interpreted very extensively, or alternatively that, because of a chain reaction, self-defence can lead to violent and uncontrollable events. France's final argument against the limitation of Security Council powers, or the extension of those of the General Assembly, underlined the danger of a conflict of powers between UN organs. This was the case in the Congo, when United Nations forces were used to put down the Katanga secession. Moreover, it is possible that a difference of judgment concerning a situation could lead to doubts as to the nature of the original mandate given to a force, certain States considering that it involved putting an end to aggression whilst others envisaged only a simple policing action.

For all these reasons, France's position, as expounded in 1965, amounts to the clearest of affirmations that

> actions referred to in Article 11, paragraph 2 cover not only the measures provided for in Articles 41 and 42 of Chapter VII of the Charter, but also any measure taken to create a military or non-military force responsible for intervention within or against a State, whether or not the State consents or the effective use of force is theoretically limited to restricted or exceptional cases. This definition leaves aside observation, surveillance or fact-finding operations.[10]

In sum, for France, any deployment of armed personnel for reasons other than observation and investigation must come under the exclusive power of the Security Council.

In addition, France has set out its position as regards the "residual powers" of the General Assembly and the extent of its powers under Article 14 of the Charter to "recommend measures for the peaceful adjustment of any situation." In this respect "measures such as border observation, truce or armistice supervision, mediation, conciliation, investigation or fact-finding are peace-keeping operations which the General Assembly has the right to recommend to the interested parties, either directly or through the Security Council."[11]

Another constitutional problem concerns force composition.[12] Current wisdom emphasizes the need for extreme prudence to ensure that the use of force by the United Nations will be in the interests of peace and not those of one or a group of States. Thus, troops and the command structure must be supplied by all three major groups of States, the East, the West, and the "neutrals." In this perspective, the permanent members of the Security Council appear suspect and, without being excluded (especially in future operations), their contributions to peace-keeping operations are not sought after. In fact, for a long time, France did not participate in peace-keeping operations. Except for its numerically modest contribution to UNTSO and its participation in the Korean war, it was not until 1978, with the creation of UNIFIL in Southern Lebanon, that France furnished any contingents.[13] In recent years France has come around to substantial participation, for example in Cambodia and former Yugoslavia.

The French position, once laid before the Committee of 33, was then explained and developed before the French Parliament, both at the government's initiative and in response to parliamentary questions. In any case, the position leaves no room for ambiguity and could be summed up as "the Charter, the whole Charter, and nothing but the Charter." Thus, the Minister of Foreign Affairs was able to declare before the National Assembly that "the role of expressing international public opinion falls upon the General Assembly, through its discussions and recommendations. If necessary, it is the Security Council which makes decisions";[14] and that "in fact, such actions were wisely placed under the sole responsibility of the Security Council, and the often quoted resolution which we improvised during the 1950 crisis has not undermined this rule."[15] Finally, in his answer to an MP's written question, the Minister of Foreign Affairs declared that

> to define our policy regarding the question of a permanent UN military force, one must refer to the provisions of the Charter. In Articles 43 et al. it sets up a

mechanism through which the Member States of the Organization provide the Security Council with all the armed forces which it may need to undertake any action deemed necessary to restore international peace and security, in so far as they have been threatened (Chapter VII) ... Concerning the military aspects of these operations, the French Government considers that the only solution is to put the relevant Articles of the Charter into effect ... In any case, it would be illogical and unrealistic to attempt to define the practical form of the aid given to the Organization by Member States for a permanent UN force without having first determined which organ has the power to launch and maintain peace-keeping operations. In this respect, we consider that the search for an agreement on the distribution of power between the Security Council and the General Assembly should be a priority. The distribution should be that which is set out in the United Nations Charter, which gives the Security Council sole power to decide on action including the use of force.[16]

Overall, French policy regarding the "constitutional" aspects of the Charter, as brought out by the first major financial crisis of the Organization twenty years after its creation, shows a desire for conformity with principles already defended in San Francisco. In effect, in 1945, during debate on Chapter VIII (which became Chapter VII in the final text), the French delegation had underlined the particular importance it attached to the work of the committee requested to study coercive measures. During a session on 10 June 1945, the French representative recalled that all of the amendments he had presented with the aim of strengthening the collective security system (to which France was most attached) were aimed at "reinforcing the effectiveness and the speed of action of the Council."[17]

France's present position: Improving the original system, now stabilized

In more recent years, France's interest in peace-keeping questions led it to propose a summit meeting of the Security Council, which was held on 31 January 1992, at the Head of State and Government level. President François Mitterrand's speech shows that French doctrine on respect for the Charter remains unchanged despite the totally new international political context. The President observed that after having been "blocked for a long time, from now on, all the provisions of the Charter may now be used and must be put into effect."[18] François Mitterrand thus called for the application of the whole of the Charter, including Chapter VII, dealing with regional agreements which "must no longer be put to one side."[19]

As a result of this summit, the Secretary-General was requested to prepare *An Agenda for Peace*[20]. The *Agenda*, published on 17 June 1992, and the *Supplement to An Agenda for Peace* of 3 January 1995,[21] which complements the first version whilst deviating on a certain number of points, have received reactions from States at the express request of the Secretary-General. On both occasions, France has been led to clarify its policy on the subject, characterized by the clearly affirmed will for involvement in actions in favour of peace. From then on, the accent has been placed much less on respect for the Charter than was the case in the past, as this is no longer under threat today. The fundamental balance between the General Assembly and the Security Council is now respected, since the revitalization of Chapter VII. The pre-eminence of the Council is clearly established and its managerial function can only satisfy France. Finally, certain provisions which had remained dead letters until now, such as Chapter VIII, have been used in recent crises. France now places greater emphasis on reinforcing the existing organs or improving their working conditions. This was the principal aim of the *aide-mémoire* dated 28 July 1993 setting out the French response to *An Agenda for Peace*.

The French reaction to An Agenda for Peace

The French *aide-mémoire* recommends strengthening the means of the Secretariat's civilian and military divisions, accompanied by improved information services for contributing States concerning the ongoing status of missions. On the military side, it insists on the need for more far-reaching military planning, as it would appear that the "the military planning function is as crucial today as political follow-up on the various conflicts in existence."[23] No mention is made of the Military Staff Committee, the reactivation of which is clearly no longer on the agenda at the United Nations, but the *aide-mémoire* does say that "there should be a gradual establishment of a new structure attached to the Secretariat and made up of officers with sound planning experience."[24] France also suggests developing contacts and exchanges of opinions between the United Nations and multilateral politico-military organizations such as NATO and the Western European Union (WEU), which already have experience in this area. Such relations would be of particular interest in cases where these organizations might be called upon to intervene in a theatre of operations at UN request. The case of the former Yugoslavia naturally comes to mind.

Politically, France recommends the strengthening of political control over the preparation of peace-keeping operations (including, for example, sending fact-finding missions), but also over their implementation. Notably, France is very much in favour of generalizing the Secretary-General's practice of sending a special representative, chosen after consultations with the parties to the conflict and the Security Council, to coordinate the different components of the operation (civil, military, and humanitarian) and keep the Secretary-General and the Security Council informed on a regular basis. The representative would also have power to coordinate relations with regional organizations (which should be encouraged), although the Secretary General's representative would retain over-all responsibility for the operation, the representatives of regional organizations and security agreements acting under his or her authority.

With a view to guaranteeing a clear mandate, the *aide-mémoire* proposes that the peace-keeping operation's "founding" resolutions specify the end political goals of the operation and that "stage" goals also be set out in the mandate.

Finally, as a State with special responsibilities owing to the relative impor-tance of its participation in peace-keeping operations, France would like to organize informal consultations with other countries having comparable respon-sibilities, so as to reflect on the important problems confronting contributing countries as a result of current developments in operations and their increasing complexity. From the French point of view, two subjects in particular should be given special attention: the question of finance (which should be broached with the Volcker–Ogata report as a starting point) and the question of the security of personnel on missions, including the sanctions likely to be applied against those responsible for aggression against personnel serving with the United Nations. The findings of such an informal group could then be passed on to the Secretary-General, the Security Council, and the General Assembly.

The French reaction to the Supplement to An Agenda for Peace

A second French *aide-mémoire*, in response to the Secretary-General's *Supple-ment to An Agenda for Peace*, was published on 30 January 1996.[25] The new document complements the 1993 *aide-mémoire* and, arguing along the lines of the *Agenda*, presents a number of proposals regarding the United Nations' rapid reaction capacity and the strengthening of the Military Staff.

France accepts the categories set out in the *Agenda* and its supplement (preventive diplomacy and peacemaking, peace-keeping, post-conflict peace-building, and enforcement action) but proposes to add the case of "operations that are deployed before a conflict has ended and are intended to restore peace or moderate the conflict by methods that involve both securing the parties' consent (principally through negotiation) and constraint (to ensure that safe areas or the free movement of humanitarian convoys are respected, for example)."[26] The specificity of these operations, of which the Rwandan Operation Turquoise is an example, results from the fact that they take place even though the conflict has not ended or is not even in the process of winding down, as is the case for traditional peace-keeping operations. These operations cannot be neutral because, by their nature, they seek to modify the behaviour of the adversaries (or at least one of them). Consent to such operations has not, thus, been obtained and only comes about, little by little, as a result of negotiations. In the meantime, the use of force may be necessary to impose aspects which have not been accepted, if not the simple presence of United Nations troops. Such operations must, thus, be based on Chapter VII and be conceived so as to allow the use of force if necessary without being limited to defensive action. They involve high risks, notably the possibility of escalation going as far as coercive military action to impose peace, and must, thus, be entrusted to well-trained and experienced troops.[27] Nor can such operations be multiplied and the Secretary-General must thus make choices.

In addition, the *aide-mémoire* recommends strengthening the capacity of the United Nations' Military Staff. Major efforts have been made to develop the General Secretariat's organizational structure, that of the Department of Peace-Keeping Operations in particular. On the other hand, in the French view, the capacity of the Military Staff is insufficient to make any useful contribution to the elaboration of a definition of the Security Council's role or allow its implementation. Without going into the French *aide-mémoire*'s detailed analysis of this aspect, it is sufficient to note that the proposal specifies a number of scenarios for intervention as soon as a crisis likely to lead to a United Nations intervention develops. Whenever an operation is envisaged, it recommends systematically sending a team into the field, made up of members of the planning

cell of the Department of Peace-Keeping Operations and a unit from a State
showing an interest in the operation. France declares itself ready to place such a
planning unit at the United Nations' disposal within 48 hours.

Finally, the *aide-mémoire* insists on the need to improve command structures.
To this end, an improvement in the efficiency of military staff and the personnel
of the Situation Room of the Department of Peace-Keeping Operations is
necessary. Better coordination of the civil and military components of operations
is equally important. In this respect, it is clearly essential in all cases for the
Secretary-General to name a special representative with authority over all aspects
of the operation.

Beyond their technical proposals, the two French *aides-mémoire* are proof of
both the continuity and the renewal of French foreign policy regarding the
United Nations. The continuity is marked by the fact that all the proposals aim to
develop the peace-keeping role of the constitutional organs, primarily that of the
principal organ, the Security Council. The renewal lies in the fact that, having
kept out of such operations (especially hostile to those deemed unconstitutional),
France is now deeply involved in both their organization and implementation. As
noted above, this attitude is coherent in so far as peace-keeping operations are
now organized under the control of a Security Council more powerful than ever
(to such an extent that voices are now being raised asking whether a judicial
review of its acts should be permitted),[28] now that Chapters VII and VIII of the
Charter have been brought out of their earlier slumber.

Understandably, in addition to the reactions addressed to the United Nations
(at its request) in the *aides-mémoire*, the French role in peace-keeping operations
has been the subject of a number of important internal studies destined for the
constitutional authorities of the State. Three such studies merit further analysis:

• the Trucy report of 1994, "French participation in peace-keeping operations";[29]
• the Defence White Paper, 1994;[30]
• the 1995 Raimond report, "The policy of intervention in conflicts: Elements of
  French doctrine."[31]

The Trucy Report, 1994

From a legal and constitutional point of view, the Trucy Report underlines the
need to catalogue actions so as to distinguish clearly to which chapter of the
Charter they are related. The exercise is not purely theoretical; it also affects

the success of the operation and the security of the participants. It is thus advisable not to confuse two distinct tasks. On one hand, there are tasks which fall within the limits of peace-keeping: "impartial action, founded on the consent of the parties, expressing a sort of armed diplomacy; in such pacifying action, only self-defence justifies opening fire." On the other hand, there are tasks which are part of "enforcing a given mission, such as those provided for in Bosnia and Somalia, based on Chapter VII ... this is military action involving, if necessary, taking sides so as to accomplish the mission, opposing those who impede it and using force, as needed, with appropriate arms."[32] Without doubt, as the report points out, the founding legal texts should be appropriate to the factual situation. Thus, if contingents are equipped for participation in a peace-keeping or humanitarian operation, they cannot be transformed abruptly into peace enforcement troops just because a Security Council resolution so decides. Owing to its strong present engagement in UN theatres of operations, France is naturally sensitive to legal ambiguities whose practical effects give rise, at best, to powerlessness and, at worst, to insecurity and humiliation. It is thus fundamental to determine the appropriate legal framework clearly, in advance, and to organize the contingents with respect to such framework without subsequent backsliding.

From a doctrinal point of view, the Trucy Report observes the time-honoured practice of the Scandinavian countries in such operations, a practice deeply imbued with concern for a neutrality and impartiality capable of leading to a form of "statism."[33] He emphasizes the interest shown by the Anglo-Saxons for the new generations of peace-keeping operations and their efforts aimed at bringing out a body of related doctrine through various events, reports, and conferences.[34]

Consequently, Trucy deplores France's relative lack of dynamism in its overall reflection on peace-keeping operations, despite numerous academic conferences in France in the last few years.[35] In fact, these conferences have not had any great resonance outside the academic world and, in any case, their aim was not to reflect French official policy. In a way, however, Senator Trucy's wish has been granted by the publication of the Defence White Paper and the Information Report by MP and former Foreign Affairs Minister Jean-Bernard Raimond.

The 1994 Defence White Paper

Whilst, naturally, only part of the 1994 Defence White Paper deals with peace-keeping operations, it still highlights a number of legal principles and raises some doctrinal issues in the matter. French participation in peace-keeping operations is directly linked to its permanent membership of the Security Council, but also to its attachment to the democratic values which must be defended as a guarantee of stability and respect for International law.

Fidelity to the Charter system is stressed, and the White Paper recalls that "the Security Council is the only international authority with power to initiate coercive or forceful measures with regard to a State, except for measures of individual or collective self-defence under Article 51 of the Charter."[36] Consequently, "action by France as a permanent member of the Security Council must seek to strengthen its influence, permit it to face increased responsibilities, thus aiding the progress of the legal principles it hopes to promote in the international community."[37]

New risks have appeared in the world and others have become more acute, for example as a result of the proliferation of arms of mass destruction, and France considers that it is up to the Security Council to find the means of facing them. Following the example of other official documents, the White Paper recommends improving the assistance (particularly military) which may be provided to the Security Council. It also notes the need to take account of the increased complexity of the Security Council's tasks compared with the first operations of the Blue Helmets. The mandates have become much wider, as they extend to State restoration operations, whereas the means have become more restrictive owing to the more frequent resort to Chapter VII. Even so, the White Paper considers that "the more natural framework for action undertaken by the UN remains peacekeeping through the use of all consensual means of peaceful settlement (Chapter VI of the Charter)."[38]

Following this perspective, the White Paper sets out three French policy orientations:

(i) The first priority is to assure the political authority of the Security Council over missions placed "under the authority" of the United Nations. This is an expression apparently applicable to a wide range of solutions, from operations directly run by the United Nations to those undertaken "on behalf of" or in execution of a "mandate" from the United Nations.

(ii) The second priority is to strengthen "the military expertise placed at the Security Council's disposition"[39] since the failure of the Military Staff Committee system.[40]

(iii) Finally, the participation of French units in United Nations operations must be subject to precise political and organizational conditions.

In the implementation of these orientations, "France desires that the Security Council exercises its authority and its capacity for political control at all stages of an operation: conception and approval of the mandate, major implementation stages and supervision of its execution."[41]

According to the White Paper, in some cases, crisis management may be handed over to a regional organization (in which case Chapter VIII of the Charter will be applied) or a military organization such as NATO or the WEU, which would be responsible for the military execution of a political responsibility which remains in the hands of the Secretary-General or his special representative.

The Raimond report

The report by J.-B. Raimond, MP and former Minister of Foreign Affairs, tabled by the Foreign Affairs Committee of the National Assembly on 23 February 1995, completes the legal analysis of a number of points related to French policy on peace-keeping operations.

The factual findings and the evolution related in the Raimond report do not differ from previous analyses although the vision is undoubtedly more subtle. Thus, the report recalls that the improved workings of the Security Council cannot be considered as given definitively. Russia used its veto in 1993 for the first time since 1984 (as the USSR) regarding funding for the UN Force in Cyprus, then again in 1994 to stop the adoption of a resolution which would be unfavourable to the Serbs,[42] and mention must be made of the discretion with which the United Nations treats anything concerning the former USSR.

The report "seeks an intervention doctrine"[43] and attempts to bring out a number of criteria. In international conflicts (apart from cases where France, like any other State, may have some particular interest in intervening), the report expresses the idea that, being a great power and a permanent member of the Security Council, France has "abstract and speculative" interests to defend.[44] This evokes a sort of "general interest" of the international community in the defence of human rights, international legality, and regional balance.[45]

In principle, on the other hand, internal conflicts are excluded from the sphere of activity of the international community, owing both to the principle of non-intervention and the difficulty in judging the responsibility of protagonists acting within their own borders. Nevertheless, the report emphasizes that "it would be false to believe that our democracies can witness such violence without danger."[46] The idea is that the values inherent in the social contract among democracies would be imperilled if the fundamental principles of our society were to be put in question in such a way. Chain reactions of destabilization could occur in a region as a result of a purely internal conflict such that "French policy cannot accept the *a priori* refusal to intervene in cases of internal conflict or civil war."[47]

United Nations authorization is one of the prerequisites for intervention listed. In effect, the report considers that intervention is conditional upon legitimacy and that this "can only be evaluated with respect to the grand principles which support our concept of international law, most of which have been defined by the United Nations, the only Organization able to claim to represent the whole of the international community."[48] Undoubtedly this analysis, which mixes questions of legitimacy and legality and confuses conformity with international law and the principles of the United Nations, merits discussion, particularly the final aspect, in so far as it seems to affirm that "the Security Council *is* the law," to paraphrase John Foster Dulles,[49] or, at least, that it is capable of "stating the law,"[50] thus assimilating international law to a sort of "derived law" of the United Nations. However, this rather rapid analysis permits the subsequent affirmation to the effect that the prerequisite of United Nations authorization "is a guarantee for France that no intervention may be undertaken without its approval, due to its veto over Security Council decisions."[51]

Finally, the Raimond report insists repeatedly on an important motive for French participation in United Nations peace-keeping operations: the need to take into account the humanitarian dimension of conflicts, whether they be international or internal. It is true that humanitarian preoccupation has been seen as a "French speciality," notably through the concept of the "duty to intervene" which had some success when first put forward, but which has already begun to ebb in favour of the more sober and less provocative "assistance to victims." Whatever the exact status of the concept, it is true that the humanitarian component of a number of recent operations, for example in Somalia and Bosnia, was fundamental. It is, thus, quite natural that France should have been present.

The strong French involvement in peace-keeping operations cannot, however, be reduced to a simple evolution in diplomatic concepts. In fact, such major participation in foreign theatres of operations naturally has consequences for the French internal order, especially for constitutional and legislative provisions with respect to the authorization and control of activities putting human lives in the balance, leading to budgetary costs and directly determining both the means and the influence of France's role in world affairs.

Constitutional problems created by peace-keeping operations within the French legal system

It must be noted here that the French Parliament, largely excluded from such external activities from the beginning, still plays only a relatively modest part in the process of initiation and supervision, despite the development and diversification of peace-keeping operations. In any case, the government has no specific obligation towards the Parliament in this domain. Of course, events may impose a need for rapidity or discretion incompatible with the extended deadlines and publicity to which parliamentary debates can lead. An incident may arise when Parliament is not in session without the calling of an extraordinary session being justified; although the Constitutional amendment of 4 August 1995, which establishes a single session from October to June, does not exclude the possibility of supplementary sessions (new Art. 28). These reasons are not, however, a sufficient explanation. When the situation prevailing in other countries (notably in Scandinavia) is observed, this partial exclusion of national representatives seems surprising.

Constitutional provisions

In fact, the French Constitution of 4 October 1958 provides for no case of use of the armed forces in foreign theatres of operations other war. Article 35, which provides that "declarations of war shall be authorized by Parliament," reaffirms a republican and democratic principle requiring a "reasoned declaration of war" before commencing hostilities. This principle is well established in France, having been included in all constitutions since the Revolution and confirmed in the third Convention of La Haye in 1907.

The rule is only partly observed in practice, however, and in a world where war has been outlawed, it seems a mere historical survival. It is clearly not adapted to current conflicts, whether it be their nature (they are no longer wars in terms of international law and Article 35 of the French Constitution) or their resolution (which, if it involves the use of force, falls under Chapter VII of the United Nations Charter). This leaves open the case of self-defence, which may justify the resort to war in conformity with international law and which, in terms of French constitutional law, is subject to Article 35. Even so, self-defence requires immediate action so as to contain or push back the invader until such time as the Security Council, having been informed, may take over. The rapidity of the victim State's reaction may even be seen as an element in impeding a further deterioration or extension of the conflict that would make a settlement more difficult. Is such a rapid response compatible with the inevitable delays required by parliamentary authorization under Article 35? Should the invader be allowed to advance while both Chambers of Parliament conclude their debates and authorize the resort to war? All in all, if Article 35 merits conservation for its symbolic and historical weight, it should at least be updated. As will be seen, a number of initiatives have been taken to this end.

The other constitutional provisions which need to be taken into consideration are Article 15, dealing with the President's duties,[52] and Article 20, paragraph 2, which provides that the Government "has at its disposal the Administration and the Armed Forces."

Constitutional practice: the absence of parliamentary authorization

The habitual distribution of powers between the President of the Republic and the government due to the dual leadership of the French Executive leads to uncertainty regarding the appropriate provisions to apply. Concerning war as such, to whom is parliamentary authorization given?[53] Undoubtedly to the government, as Article 35 is part of Chapter V of the Constitution, entitled "Relations between the Parliament and the Government" and because the Government "has at its disposal ... the Armed Forces." This also seems logical in the sense that authorization is given to the Government, the organ which is responsible before Parliament. Even so, the practice of the Fifth Republic with respect to presidential power (especially concerning nuclear weapons) must be taken into account.[54]

This aspect of all French Constitutions has been liberally interpreted[55] and, in any case, none of the provisions is strictly applicable to peace-keeping operations. Consequently, whilst such important decisions cannot be made without the agreement of the President, they are generally the subject of government decisions with the direct involvement of the Ministries of Foreign Affairs and Defence. Legally speaking, however, these decisions do not seem to require any particular formalities, nor are they treated any differently than other decisions involving French participation in United Nations activities or organizing its relations with that Organization (see above, chapter 1, p. 28).

This results in unfortunate "legal ambiguity" or, at the very least, the lack of any specific procedure permitting MPs to be directly and systematically associated with decisions as important as participation in peace-keeping operations. As a result, a number of remedies have been formulated.

Reform proposals

Before examining the proposals, it should be noted that Parliament has been brought in on a decision in some cases, although not systematically. Such a situation arose when the Government was obliged to obtain Parliamentary authorization in accordance with Article 53 of the French Constitution for its approval of an international agreement related to a multinational and observer force in the Sinai. Legally, this was a rather strange agreement, consisting of two exchanges of letters dated 18 and 20 March 1982 and signed by the French Minister of Foreign Relations, and an "Authorization." As regards the protocol of 3 August 1981, the Director General of the multinational force was designated by Egypt and Israel. The aim in creating the multinational force was to make up for the impossibility of constituting a United Nations force to ensure the application of the peace treaty between Egypt and Israel. Once parliamentary authorization had been granted, France participated alongside nine other countries, initially providing 42 personnel and varied equipment.

This case is, however, outside the strict ambit of this study. First, strictly speaking, it did not involve a peace-keeping operation but a multinational force substituted for a peace-keeping operation, even if the two cases are comparable from the point of view of the rules of engagement for French troops overseas. Secondly, the parliamentary involvement was necessary because the aims of the pre-existing agreement required parliamentary authorization under Article 53 of the Constitution.

Amongst the proposals aimed at improving and completing the French constitutional system so as to take account of peace-keeping operations, the most important is the Constitutional Amendment Bill for the purpose of updating Article 35, tabled on 12 December 1991 by Senator Jean Lecanuet and other centrist senators. The accompanying declaration stated that "the fact that the elected representatives of the Nation are not involved in the decision-making process regarding the deployment of military forces outside its own borders cannot be tolerated in a democracy,"[56] whether or not the conflict concerned amounts to war. The proposal, which was never debated, preserved the text of Article 35, despite its mainly theoretical nature, so as to respect republican tradition, but added a supplementary paragraph which read, "Parliament is kept informed of all foreign interventions by French military forces including the implementation and conclusion of the action." There was no question of authorization but only of information. The text represented a compromise between the need to involve Parliament in such operations and that of preserving executive prerogatives, especially those of the President, so as not to reduce the efficiency of military operations and the credibility of France's deterrent capability.[57]

At about the same time, two other bills were tabled by MPs dealing with the specific case of foreign interventions by the French army in countries with which France had signed co-operation agreements.[58] It was proposed that such interventions be subject to the prior agreement of Parliament. However, neither of the bills ever came up for discussion.

That is why, in its report to the President of 15 February 1993, the Consultative Committee on the review of the Constitution, chaired by Professor Georges Vedel, proposed to remedy the situation by adding a second paragraph to Article 35, providing that "all foreign interventions by French Armed Forces shall be the subject of a Declaration before Parliament, no later than eight days after engagement. The Declaration is followed by a debate. If Parliament is not in session, it meets for this purpose."[59] In other words, the Committee's proposal would have had the effect of formalizing the practice followed during the Gulf conflict, which will be presented below.

None of these proposals has ever been adopted, however, with the result that the control over French participation in peace-keeping operations by its elected representatives remains unsystematic.

Parliamentary desire for a precise legal framework permitting the exercise of control over important operations falling clearly within its power is understandable. It should be emphasized, however, that such control can also be achieved by following the habitual procedures set out in the Constitution and the regulations of the two Chambers of Parliament dealing with the responsibility of the Government before the National Assembly, government declarations of general policy before the Senate, or simple information-gathering by Parliament through questions. Such procedures have in fact been used in relation to the deployment of French troops in United Nations peace-keeping operations or operations conducted "under its responsibility," but not systematically.

The possible use of general information gathering and control procedures

Parliamentary information-gathering and control over the Executive are indispensable functions of all representative democracy, although the methods of exercising these prerogatives vary with respect to the circumstances and the subject matter of the case in question.

Control by putting government responsibility in question

During the Gulf crisis, Parliamentary power was debated at length. During the session of 12 December 1990, before the beginning of military operations against Iraq but after the adoption of Security Council resolution 678, 29 November 1990, authorizing the use of "all necessary means to uphold and implement Security Council resolution 660," Mr Jean-François Deniau, MP, questioned the Prime Minister on the relevance to the Gulf crisis of Article 35 of the Constitution, since the crisis was likely to become a war if Saddam Hussein failed to bow to Security Council commands within the prescribed time limits. Mr Deniau considered that France thus found itself in a "logic of war," taking up the expression made popular by President Francois Mitterand, who had contrasted the "logic of war" with the "logic of peace," since Resolution 678 laid down an ultimatum upon the expiration of which force could be used. In his opinion, the fact that there was no precedent for the use of Article 35 did not exclude its application in this case. In his answer, the Prime Minister developed a double-barrelled legal reasoning. In the first place, he observed that the decision to use force fell within presidential power due to his role as Commander-in-Chief of the Armed Forces (Art. 15) and as guarantor of the respect of treaties (Art. 5). The

Prime Minister then indicated that, if force were to be used against Iraq, such military action would not, formally, be subject to a declaration of war. Effectively,

France has never envisaged any action outside the framework of the United Nations and its Charter, Chapter VII of which explicitly provides for the use of armed force, even if, in certain cases and on precise conditions (set out in its resolutions), the Council may leave the initiative to Member States. In international law, as in French law, that is, legally speaking, it would not be a question of war declared by one State against another but of collective security action taken under Chapter VII of the Charter. The President alone has power to decide the timing, conditions and level of any French engagement, subject, naturally, to the Prime Minister's obligation to account to you for such decisions and assume responsibility under Article 21 of the Constitution.[60]

This reasoning is debatable, given the questions of legality raised by the Gulf War,[61] especially with respect to the "initiative" capability given to "certain Members" within the framework of Chapter VII. It remains that the Gulf action was no more a war, within the meaning of Article 35 of the Constitution, than any other current conflict. That is why, when the question was next raised before Parliament, it was during an extraordinary session of the National Assembly expressly convoked just before the beginning of the military operation, not for the purpose of requesting "authorization" under Article 35 of the Constitution, but simply to keep Parliament informed of the situation.

At the beginning of the military operation in the Persian Gulf, despite the gravity of the situation and the uncertainty as to its evolution, the French military engagement had not been preceded, for the reasons already discussed, by a formal declaration of war under Article 35 of the Constitution. Consequently, the Head of State decided that the Parliament should be fully and ceremoniously associated with this large-scale military action requiring strong national cohesion, as is the case during all a country's darkest hours. Accordingly, the President called an extraordinary session of Parliament on 16 January 1991 with the following agenda: the reading to the Parliament of a message from the President followed by a declaration by the Government on its Middle East policy.

In his message, the Head of State recalled that he had addressed the people of France frequently to keep them informed of the evolution of the situation and that the Prime Minister had met regularly with majority and minority leaders of both Chambers of Parliament to explain government action in this grave crisis.

This procedure, although not formally recognized, constituted an informal, simple, and effective means of keeping Parliament informed.

The President added that "the use of armed force to compel Iraq to leave Kuwait is now legitimate. That is why I will order the use of all military means required for French participation in the implementation of the Security Council's resolutions."[62] This presentation clearly designated the legal framework for the use of force, not a war in the classical sense employed by Article 35 of the Constitution, but rather the implementation of obligations arising out of the Charter or following upon action decided by United Nations organs.

If procedural rules do not require parliamentary authorization, the matters dealt with require it to be informed so as to permit control. To allow this role to be exercised in full, after the Prime Minister had presented his Government's declaration and participated in the subsequent debate, he engaged the responsibility of the Government under Article 49, paragraph 1 of the Constitution so as to allow a vote. The declaration was approved massively, by 523 for and 43 against, confirming the wide parliamentary consensus on the subject. The same conclusion may be drawn from the way in which the Government's declaration of general policy was approved by the Senate under Article 49, paragraph 4.[63]

It is to be regretted that Parliament is only invited to give its opinion during crises as serious as that of the Gulf War, while French participation in other peace-keeping operations escapes any direct or systematic control. The control by French elected representatives occurs thus in an indirect way and "after the event," through questions addressed to the Government or the vote on the budget.

Information through parliamentary questions

Parliamentary questions, with or without debate, have been addressed to the Government fairly regularly on all major peace-keeping operations, as for military action outside the United Nations framework (Chad, for example) or on its fringes (French participation in the multinational forces and in Lebanon). In the same way, the situation in the Persian Gulf was the subject of numerous requests for information in the form of questions followed by long debates at every critical stage of the crisis, in addition to the President's message and the statement by the Prime Minister after the beginning of the military operation; especially after the adoption of Resolution 678, as it appeared at that time that clarification was needed regarding "the overlapping logics of war and peace."[64] Even before the major turning point in the crises represented by Resolution 678, the Minister of Foreign Affairs had already intervened 11 times in response to parliamentary questions, at times even outside the official Wednesday afternoon sessions devoted to questions to the Government.

Former Yugoslavia was also the subject of numerous parliamentary questions, as much on the aspects of the conflict related to the parties themselves (the evocation of genocide, massacres, ethnic cleansing, massive violations of human rights, the political and economic situation, etc.) as directly on French policy and interests. This required the Minister of Foreign Affairs to explain or justify a number of French political and diplomatic initiatives. Moreover, given the size of the French contribution to the Blue Helmets, the Government was frequently required to give details on the physical condition of the French soldiers[65] and information concerning the more dramatic incidents such as the taking hostage of Blue Helmets by the Bosnian Serbs.[66]

The effect of these questions is, at the same time, to inform Parliament, permit (non-binding) control over the Government and suggest new directions or action, as was the case for the former Yugoslavia.

Information from government communiqués
The weekly government communiqués provided for in Article 132 of the Regulations of the National Assembly may sometimes be followed by a debate. If so, each political group represented in Parliament may speak for 30 minutes. If there is no debate, a sole speaker may respond to the Government. In no case may a vote take place. Thus a communiqué, aimed at informing the Assembly and permitting more efficient control, cannot lead to a censure motion against the Government.

This procedure, used widely for questions of foreign affairs, has equally been used to control over the conditions in which France participates in peace-keeping operations.

On 27 August 1990, during the first weeks of the Gulf crisis, the Prime Minister made a declaration, followed by a long debate.[68] In the same way, on 19 March 1991, after the end of the military operation, the Government made another declaration before the Assembly followed by a debate.[69] The summary of these two sessions takes up more than 36 pages of the *Journal Officiel*, the different points of view having been expounded at length.

In this respect, as is often the case in matters of French foreign policy, the opinions of the majority and those of the opposition are largely concurrent with respect to decisions made about United Nations peace-keeping operations.[70] Apart from "snide comments" and various skirmishes, the Government receives broad opposition support in the conduct of a policy marked by its continuity. This is confirmed on those occasions when a formal vote is required, such as votes of confidence in the Government.

2 Special legislation

Owing to the recent development of France's participation in peace-keeping and related operations, specific legislation has been passed to regulate certain aspects which have become more important in consequence. One of the most significant examples is that of former Yugoslavia, where the important French military presence raised unavoidable questions of responsibility. Damage caused or suffered by French troops on United Nations peace-keeping operations in former Yugoslavia falls under the United Nations reparations system. It is outside the jurisdiction of French regulations and will not be examined here.[71]

Reparation of non-contractual damage

On the other hand, with respect to the French military participation in IFOR since its creation on 20 December 1995, special provision has been made to indemnify non-contractual damage caused or suffered by French troops. The major characteristic is a geographical decentralization designed to increase efficiency.

The reparation of damage caused or suffered in this context is regulated by an Order issued by the Armed Forces Staff on 14 May 1996.[72] The general organizational principles aim to designate a single administrative level to deal with all claims for damages arising out of IFOR. This sole local level is aimed at simplifying, speeding up, and homogenizing the procedure for resolving claims.

The claims mechanism is thus made up of only two levels. The central level (the legal proceedings and reparations bureau of the General Administration Department in the Defence Ministry: DAG/CX) has responsibility for aerial and maritime damage. The local level, at the head of which is a Joint Armed Forces Commander with power to pay damages claims, is set up to investigate and settle claims. To this end, a bureau, DOMIFORFRANCE, has been set up covering Bosnia and Herzegovina, Croatia, and the Federal Republic of Yugoslavia. The bureau has jurisdiction over all non-contractual damage other than that involving principles of air and sea law (degradation of landing strips or ports, for instance) within certain monetary limits above which the central bureau has jurisdiction.[73] In addition, minor material damage may be examined following a free, simplified procedure allowing the Bureau to indemnify the victims of damage arising from the personal fault of French members of IFOR and unconnected with their service. Legal action may then be taken against the perpetrator of the act. The Order of 14 May 1996 gives DOMIFORFRANCE a general mission to attempt to reach out-of-court settlements in all cases. A matter may be referred to DOMIFOR-FRANCE in two ways, regardless of whether French forces were perpetrators or victims of the damage. First, it is imperative that all reports of accidents involving the French contingent established by the Provost Marshal be transferred to the Bureau for filing. Second, there is a centralized process for claims by the local population with respect to damage caused by the national contingents of IFOR. All such claims are gathered by the Ministry of the Interior of the host State and transferred to the Claims Bureau of IFOR, which distributes them to the specialized structures of each State, DOMIFORFRANCE in France's case. It is this bureau which investigates all matters transferred to it through these two channels. As far as possible, out-of-court settlement is preferred.[74]

The Order stresses the need "to act with prudence. If it appears that local laws cannot be applied, it will be necessary to rely on the rules applicable when dealing with similar damages claims in France. Of course, the level of compensation offered must be appropriate to the local context."

The allocation of "veteran's cards"

Another concrete example of the practical consequences of increased French involvement in peace-keeping operations is the recent amendment of the regulations regarding the right to a "veteran's card." The general conditions of allocation of the card, set by Law No. 93-7, 4 January 1993,[75] have been complemented by a number of regulations. In particular, a Decree of 12 January 1994 lists the military operations participation in which entitles soldiers to the card, including Cambodia, Lebanon, Somalia, and the former Yugoslavia.[76]

3 Stand-by agreements

The development and diversification of peace-keeping operations not having been matched by the setting up of either a United Nations Army or Military Staff Committee, it has become crucial to know upon which forces the Secretary-General may count when organizing an operation created by the Security Council.

This involves a major practical difficulty for the Secretary-General. Very often he is unable to rely upon States to contribute military personnel within a short enough period to meet the needs of the operation in question. This is one reason why substitute national or multinational forces are sometimes used. This was the case for Operation Turquoise, undertaken by the French Army in Rwanda under a Security Council mandate, because it would have taken a number of months to gather a United Nations contingent, during which time the massacres would have continued. Moreover, the two months' duration of the mandate corresponded to the period deemed necessary by the United Nations to create UNAMIR II.[77]

In these conditions, the need for a system of stand-by forces is particularly important. Numerous States have made specific promises in this regard. Nevertheless, these promises have not been systematically followed up by formal agreements.

France has not concluded any stand-by agreement with the United Nations, partly because of the need for coordination within the European Union, at least, according to the explanations proffered from time to time. This formal aspect is not, however, of any great importance, given that, on numerous occasions and in widely varying circumstances, France has declared its approval for the system of stand-by forces and made solemn promises to participate.

Such was the case when President François Mitterrand spoke before the Security Council on 31 January 1992 to propose the reactivation of the Military Staff Committee so as to give practical effect to his proposal to "place a contingent of 1,000 men at the disposition of the Secretary-General of the United Nations for peace-keeping operations at all times, within 48 hours' notice, with the possibility of doubling the number within a week".[78]

The then Minister of Foreign Affairs, Alain Juppé, confirmed this point before the National Assembly when he declared: "We have pleaded in favour of the creation of a network of stand-by forces. We have proposed placing a contingent of high-mobility forces at the Secretary-General's disposition at all times, within a very short period of notice."[79]

These ideas are taken up and clarified in the two *aide-mémoire* related to the Secretary-General's *An Agenda for Peace*, published by France on 28 July 1993[80] and 30 January 1996.[81] Through the detailed proposals formulated with respect to logistics and mobilization of personnel, they show the extent to which France is engaged henceforth in peace-keeping operations. The French note emphasizes the increasing need for United Nations interventions, making necessary a profound reform of the system of mobilizing Blue Helmets necessary.[82] In particular, it is indispensable to place rapid reaction forces at UN disposal. These "Force Units," by including a larger number of States in peace-keeping missions, would help overcome the present saturation of the capacity of regular troop-contributing countries. Furthermore, the Organization's principle of neutrality would be better respected. Nevertheless, such a parcelling-out of troops requires increased coordination and uniformity, or at least harmonization of concepts and methods, which may not be feasible in practice.

The second proposal made by the French *aide-mémoire* is the improvement of the United Nations' reaction capability by perfecting the system of stand-by units and setting up rapid reaction units. The UNAMIR II experience, only coming into operation six months after its creation by Security Council resolution, led France to make proposals aimed at allowing the Security Council to play its role and the United Nations to fulfil its mission. The French reflections thus contribute to increased efficiency of the Charter system.

The stand-by units were already foreseen in 1994, but, for them to be operational, the Secretariat must have sufficient details to be able to put together a coherent and suitable force out of the various units. Consequently, France recommended the promotion of the system amongst other States and requested the provision of more detailed information from participating countries on the units they propose. Those States with sufficient capacity should also propose command units including Military Staff elements to which officers from other States could be seconded.

Further, the French Government supports the Secretary-General's proposal to set up a rapid reaction force contained in his *Supplement to An Agenda for Peace*. The *aide-mémoire* mentions the proposal made by President Mitterrand at the Summit meeting of the Security Council on 31 January 1992 and underlines the importance of reducing time limits as much as possible, as all delay aggravates the field situation and reduces the chances of a successful operation.[83]

True, as has been said, these unilateral declarations have not been confirmed by formal engagements in the form of stand-by agreements, but such positions officially expressed by France may be considered as promises of which the legally binding nature is well established in international law.[84]

Unsurprisingly, the same ideas have flowed from the pen of the then Minister of State and Defence Minister, François Léotard, in a doctrinal book: "In order to face the new challenges of the post-Cold War period and the resulting multiplication of interventions, the rapidity of the World Organization's response to crises must be increased. In this respect, France has participated in the reflection carried out by the Secretariat aimed at creating "stand-by units."[85]

This involves creating a sort of "data bank" of peace-keeping forces which would allow the UN to intervene without delay once such a decision was made. The search for troop contributors would be quicker and the preparation period for transport and initial deployment would be significantly reduced.

To ensure that the normal exercise of national sovereignty should not be hindered, nothing would be automatic. In the last resort, troop-contributing countries would remain masters of their decisions. In October 1994, a number of countries had already indicated their willingness to participate in such a mechanism of stand-by units. On 15 July 1995, France decided to authorize the inclusion of 5000 men in the "data bank," capable of enlargement "according to needs and possibilities."

4 Cooperation in regional or bilateral frameworks

Regardless of any importance acquired by France in the conduct of peace-keeping operations, it is quite clear that it cannot act alone. In particular, its action must always be seen in the larger European context, which requires a minimum of coordination. This necessity will increase with the development of the Common Foreign and Security Policy (CFSP), even if the Maastricht Treaty takes account of the specific interests of the two members which are also permanent members of the Security Council.

During President Jacques Chirac's official visit to London in May 1996, the decision was made to look into setting up a "Franco-British High Commission for Peace-keeping", sometimes called the "High Commission" project. Despite being bilateral, the project is also situated in a European context, as it aims to promote not only the participation of these two countries in peace-keeping operations, but also that of all European countries.

Given the high degree of competence achieved by France and the United Kingdom in this domain, particularly due to the size of their participation and coordinated action in peace-keeping operations and IFOR in Bosnia, it is high time to act with more harmony and develop joint training exercises. Such co-operation could be supervised by the High Commission (Franco-British at first, but open to participation by other members of the WEU) composed of representatives of Foreign Affairs and Defence Ministries. The presidency of the High Commission would rotate and be filled by a high ranking officer or diplomat, working in both languages. The aim would be to develop a common approach to peace-keeping operations, especially concerning the use of force, through the detachment of Military Staff officers to the sections of the French and British armies involved in the planning and conduct of peace-keeping operations. This should lead to the development of common approaches to each category of peace-keeping operation, their planning and structure, the composition of the force and the means placed at their disposal, the rules of engagement, and their preparation and conduct. Finally, the High Commission would be in charge of setting up a common inter-army training programme including joint teaching sessions, documentation, internships, and military colleges.

Generally speaking, the future seems to hold a clear perspective of the likelihood of developing European cooperation in this domain. The Yugoslavian crisis required resort to existing organizations (WEU and NATO) or ad hoc mechanisms (IFOR). European cooperation will continue to move in this direction.

Notes

1. On this point see M.C. Smouts, above, and T. Tardy, "La France et l'ONU, 50 ans de relations contrastées" [France and the UN, 50 years of contrasting relations], in *Regards sur l'actualité* 215 (Paris: La Documentation française, November 1995), pp. 3ff.

2. This aspect is too often neglected in analyses of the composition and proposed reform of the Security Council. The questions of permanent membership and the veto power are, of course, the primary issues, but a secondary issue, of equally great

importance in practice and a consequence of the first, is membership not only of the primary organs (ECOSOC, ICJ) but also most of the permanent and ad hoc committees and commissions.

3. For the complete French position before the "Committee of 33," see the statements by R. Seydoux, permanent representative of France, on 17 May 1965: A/5916 Ann.21, p. 59 (A/AC.121/SR.7).

4. *Ibid.*

5. *Ibid.*

6. *Ibid.*

7. "Certain expenses of the United Nations" [Art. 17(2)] Advisory Opinion, 20 July 1962, *ICJ Reports*, 1962, p. 151.

8. On the subject of "imaginary chapters" see the stimulating variations proposed by B. Stern in: "L'évolution du rôle des Nations Unies dans le maintien de la paix et de la sécurité internationales."

9. Also, the Security Council stated that a state of internal conflict could have international consequences for the region, in Resolution 841, 16 June 1993, concerning the situation in Haiti.

10. Statement by R. Seydoux (A/AC.121/SR.7).

11. *Ibid.* para. 9.

12. E. Zoller, "Le principe de répartition géographique dans la composition des forces des Nations Unies" [The principle of geographical distribution in the composition of United Nations forces], *Annuaire français de droit international*, 1975, p. 503.

13. J. Leprette, "La France au Conseil de sécurité" [France in the Security Council], in Lewin (ed.), *La France et l'ONU depuis 1945*, pp. 174ff.

14. *Journal Officiel de l'Assemblée Nationale* [*JOAN*], 21 October, quoted in J. Charpentier, "Pratique française du droit international" [French practice of international law], *Annuaire français de droit international*, 1966, p. 914.

15. *Ibid.*

16. *Ibid.* p. 915.

17. Doc. of the United Nations Conference on International Organization, San Francisco, vol. XI, p. 43 (Doc. 943, III/5, 13 June 1945, p. 16).

18. Summit Meeting of the Security Council, New York, 31 January 1992, United Nations, p. 11, S/23500.

19. *Ibid.*

20. A/47/277–S/24111.

21. A/50/60–S/1995/1.

22. A/48/403/ Add.1–S/26450/Add.1.

23. *Ibid.* para. 5. On the military aspects, see chapter 4, below.

24. *Ibid.* para. 6.

25. A/50/869–S/1996/71.

26. *Ibid.* p. 2 (mimeographed version).

27. On the military aspects of this question, see chapter 4, below.
28. M. Bedjaoui, *Nouvel ordre mondial et contrôle de légalité des actes du Conseil de sécurité* [The New World Order and judicial review of the acts of the Security Council], Brussels: Bruylant, 1994.
29. For full reference, see above, Introduction, n.3. Senator Trucy was MP on mission, 4 August, 1993–4 February 1994. This is his second report, the first being that cited above in chapter 1, n. 29.
30. *Livre blanc sur la défense*, preface by E. Balladur (Prime Minister) and F. Leotard (Defence Minister), UGE 10/18, 1994.
31. *La politique d'intervention dans les conflits*, tabled by the Foreign Affairs Committee of the National Assembly, presented by J.-B. Raimond, MP and former Minister of Foreign Affairs, 23 February, 1995. Published in the series *Les documents d'information*, Assemblée Nationale, Commission des affaires étrangères, Rapport d'information no. 150, Paris, 1995.
32. F. Trucy, "Participation de la France aux opérations de maintien de la paix," p. 16.
33. *Ibid.* p. 21.
34. The important role played by the Ford Foundation is worth noting in this respect.
35. Among many others, one may note: B. Stern (ed.), *Les aspects juridiques de la crise et de la guerre du Golfe* [Legal aspects of the Gulf crisis and war], Paris: Montchrestien, 1991; Y. Daudet (ed.): *Aspects du système des Nations Unies dans le cadre de l'idée d'un nouvel ordre mondial* [Aspects of the UN system in the context of the concept of a new world order], Paris: Pédone, 1992; *Actualités des conflits internationaux* [Update on international conflicts], Paris: Pédone 1993; *Les Nations Unies et la restauration de l'Etat* [The UN and the restoration of States], Paris: Pédone, 1994; *La crise de Haïti (1991–1996)* [The Haiti crisis], Paris: Montchrestien, 1996; Société française pour le droit international, *Le chapitre VII de la Charte* [Chapter VII of the UN Charter], Paris: Pédone, 1995.
36. *Livre blanc sur la défense*, p. 72.
37. *Ibid.*
38. *Ibid.* p. 73.
39. *Ibid.* p. 74.
40. On this point, a report by General Cot, recommending the development of an independent mechanism to aid the Security Council in the area of evaluation and control, sets out "a call for a consultative military committee of the Security Council," noting that "compared to the Military Staff Committee provided for in the Charter, present practice has brought out different needs. Rather than a Military Staff made up of a coalition of the five permanent members of the Security Council, peace-keeping operations, as they have evolved over the last few years, show the need to provide the Security Council with an instrument capable of fulfilling numerous tasks:
    • collecting, analysing, and distributing confidential information capable of contributing to the preventive management of crisis situations;
    • providing the Security Council with detailed advice on the military implications of

decisions it might wish to make. The Council could, thus, give a consultative opinion on the military options proposed by the Secretary-General in his or her reports. It could formulate more detailed recommendations and permit more rapid consultations with troop-contributing countries so as to be sure of the availability of forces ready to be deployed. Such strictly consultative advice would allow the Council to avoid taking militarily inapplicable measures. In this respect, the consultative committee we propose has similar responsibilities to the Committee for international peace and security proposed by the Canadians;

- exercising external control over operations in the field. This last point is particularly important;
- sketching out a doctrine of the use of force."

(Fondation pour les études de défense, "Le renforcement de la capacité militaire du Conseil de sécurité" [Strengthening the military capacity of the Security Council], Report by General Cot, June 1995.

41. *Ibid.*
42. *La politique d'intervention dans les conflits*, p. 19.
43. *Ibid.* pp. 43ff.
44. *Ibid.* p. 54.
45. *Ibid.*
46. *Ibid.* p. 55.
47. *Ibid.*
48. *Ibid.*
49. "The Security Council is not a body that merely enforces agreed laws. It is Law unto itself" (John Foster Dulles, *War or Peace*, New York, 1950, quoted in Bedjaoui, *Nouvel ordre mondial ...*, p. 11.
50. Which is neither its function nor one of its powers, as Leprette points out ("La France au Conseil de sécurité," p. 171).
51. *La politique d'intervention dans les conflits*, p. 58.
52. Article 15: "The President of the Republic is the Commander-in-Chief of the armed forces. He chairs higher national defence councils and committees."
53. Both Chambers sit separately: Regulations of the National Assembly, Article 131 – vote on an express text of government origin referring to Article 35 of the Constitution; Regulations of the Senate, Article 73 – declaration by the Government followed by a vote following the procedure set out in the last paragraph of Article 49 of the Constitution (approval of a declaration of general policy).
54. Decrees (*décrets*) of 14 January 1964 and 12 June 1996 (*Journal Officiel [J.O.]* of 15 June 1996).
55. See Th. S. Renoux and M. de Villiers, *Code constitutionnel* [The Constitutional Code] (Paris: Litec, 1995), commentary on Article 35, p. 366; R. Hadas Lebel, "La cinquième République et la Guerre" [The Fifth Republic and War], *Pouvoirs* 58, 1991, pp. 5ff.
56. Senate, Report no. 173, 12 December 1991, p. 10.

57. *Ibid.* p. 13.

58. *J.O. déb. AN* 28 June 1990, p. 3143 and 13 July, 1993, p. 3301.

59. *J.O.*, 16 February 1993, p. 2545.

60. *J.O. déb. AN* 12 December 1990, p. 6749.

61. See B. Stern (ed.), *Les aspects juridiques de la crise et de la guerre du Golfe.*

62. *J.O. déb. AN* 16 January 1991, p. 3.

63. Renoux and de Villiers, *Code constitutionnel*; see also above.

64. M. Vauzelle, Chairman of the Standing Committee on Foreign Affairs, session of 5 December 1990, *J.O. déb. AN* 5 December 1990, p. 6390.

65. See, for example, the preoccupation expressed in the National Assembly during the session on 23 June 1993 over the risks to which the French contingent was exposed (*J.O. déb. AN*, p. 2096).

66. Session of 6 June 1995, statement by the Government followed by a debate (*J.O. déb. AN* 6 June 1995, p. 419); session of 14 June 1995, *J.O. déb. AN* 14 June 1995 p. 486.

67. Amongst many other examples, it is worth noting the questions addressed by Charles Millon to Prime Minister Pierre Bérégovoy, aimed at obtaining the strengthening and toughening of the military action against the Serbs (*J.O. déb. AN* 16 December 1992, p. 7307).

68. *J.O. déb. AN* 27 August 1990, p. 3214.

69. *J.O. déb. AN* 19 March 1991, p. 28.

70. Thus, for example, M. Léotard, speaking for the UDF (the Union for French Democracy, in opposition at the time), was able to tell the Prime Minister that one of the reasons for opposition support of the Government was that "the more French policy follows that of the United Nations, the more natural that the opposition should support it" (*J.O. déb. AN* 19 March 1991, p. 31).

71. Naturally the situation is completely different concerning criminal responsibility and military discipline, which are subject to the general laws and regulations applicable to French military personnel, having no aspects specific to UN peace-keeping. French soldiers are subject to the same rules of military discipline whether they serve in France or elsewhere, in traditional military action or peace-keeping operations. It should be noted, as a matter of interest, that since the passing of a law of 21 July 1982, military tribunals no longer have jurisdiction in peacetime. In such cases, the offences set out in the old Code of Military Justice of 1965 are tried by the common law courts (Art. 1 of the Code), although the trial may be organized differently. Thus, in the case of the Blue Helmets in Bosnia, criminal acts were reported by the Provost Marshal to the Attorney General, who then prosecuted before the normal criminal courts.

72. Provisional Order no. 903/DEF/EMA/OL/GEND, no. 5158/DEF/DAG/CX/3, concerning the reparation of non-contractual damage in former Yugoslavia, BOC/PP no. 24, 10 June 1996, p. 2134.

73. The monetary thresholds for the decentralized authorities were set by a decree of 27 July 1996 (Art. 2) as follows: Decisions to indemnify: 500,000 French francs [US$1 = approx. 5 FF] ; Provisional indemnities: 150,000 FF; Refusal to indemnify: unlimited; Decisions to claim liability of a third person: unlimited.

74. Concerning traffic accidents, specific rules apply due to the effect on motor vehicle insurance of the principles set out in the La Haye Convention of 4 May 1971 regarding the law applying to road traffic accidents.

75. *J.O.*, 5 January 1993, p. 250.

76. *J.O.*, 11 February 1994, p. 2364.

77. J.-C. Lafourcade, "Turquoise, une intervention militaire de restauration de la paix à but humanitaire" [Turquoise, a military intervention to restore peace with humanitarian aims], in FED, *Opérations des Nations Unies: leçons de terrain*, p. 211.

78. *Ibid.*

79. National Assembly session of 28 October 1993, *J.O. déb. AN* 28 October 1993, p. 5100.

80. A/48/403 Add.1–S/26450/ Add.1.

81. A/50/869–S/1996/71.

82. A/48/403 Add.1–S/26450/ Add.1, para. 11ff.

83. In addition, according to General Cot (in Fondation pour les études de défense, "Le renforcement de la capacité militaire du Conseil de sécurité"), "The main value of a rapid reaction force would be to give peace-keeping operations the reserves of which they may have need in some cases: in cases of violation of previously negotiated agreements, to reinforce and provide security for the Blue Helmets and the civil personnel working with them; in cases of changes to the original mandate, the peace-keeping operation being transformed into a peace enforcement mission due to the lack of cooperation of one of the parties; in cases of widened mandates such as the creation of safe zones or intervention forces."

84. International Court of Justice, Nuclear Tests Case (Australia v. France), 20 December 1974, para. 46: "One of the basic principles governing the creation and performance of legal obligations, whatever their source, is the principle of good faith. Trust and confidence are inherent in international co-operation, in particular in an age when this co-operation in many fields is becoming increasingly essential. Just as the very rule of *pacta sunt servanda* in the law of treaties is based on good faith, so also is the binding character of an international obligation assumed by unilateral declaration. Thus interested States may take cognizance of unilateral declarations and place confidence in them, and are entitled to require that the obligation thus created be expected" (Rec. 1974, p.268).

85. A. Lewin (ed.), *La France et l'ONU depuis 1945*, p. 210.

3

BUDGETARY AND FINANCIAL ASPECTS

Yves Daudet

1 French budgetary regulations

In France, the principle of yearly budgets requires the passage of a finance law every year before 31 December, the new financial year commencing on 1 January. The original budget passed in this way may later be modified by further rectifying finance laws. As for control of implementation, this occurs through the passage of a regulatory law at the end of the budget year. Accordingly, the Parliament exercises its traditional power of authorization and control over the various activities of the Executive in a classic constitutional schema involving a vote on the budget of each Ministry.[1]

2 French rules for funding peace-keeping operations

When applied to the specific case of peace-keeping operations, the situation becomes more complicated than the above presentation would seem to indicate. In the first place, two ministries are concerned by such action, Foreign Affairs, which includes the United Nations budget for peace-keeping operations, and Defence, which pays the costs of military matériel for the contingents involved in peace-keeping operations. Then, despite the regular large-scale participation of France, peace-keeping operations continue to be seen as unpredictable situations which must be dealt with out of funds not already allocated. As a presidential decision confirmed on 25 April 1978, this requires the passage of a rectifying finance law. It is true that, from one point of view, many conflicts requiring the organization of a peace-keeping operation will not have been foreseen when the budget was passed, resulting in a lack of funds to deal with them. On the other hand, it can be argued that since peace-keeping operations now constitute an aspect of French foreign policy, there is always a chance of Blue Helmets being sent to deal with a situation somewhere, such that PKOs are no longer unpredictable. Such an approach would provide the "financial equivalent" of stand-by forces.

The Trucy report of 1994 deals with this question at length and observes that "the theoretical unpredictability of peace-keeping operations destabilizes budgetary matters. They are dealt with case by case, after the event."[2] This arises because

> in principle, the annual budgets of the Defence Ministry cover the costs of the permanent presence of forces outside the mainland territory of France: the overseas Territories and Departments and certain foreign countries with which we have defence treaties. However, the budget does not normally allocate funds to cover the additional expense involved in the non-permanent deployment of forces in foreign operations of unknown length.[3]

The uncertainty and legal ambiguity is further aggravated by the fact that not only is "the political decision to initiate a foreign operation ... made with neither consideration nor knowledge of the approximate cost," but, in addition, "the legal framework of these operations is unclear, the concept of 'crisis' having no legal content." The result is that "for the Defence Ministry, so-called peace-keeping operations do not constitute a separate budgetary category. They are included in general foreign operations and share the financial cover provided for all such operations,"[4] making up an "additional" budget.

Parliament is aware of this problem. During the debate on the 1994 finance law, the spokesman for the Commission dealing with the defence budget declared that there was an urgent need to find a permanent system for financing the expenses of peace-keeping operations.[5] This preoccupation leads to another, that of identifying the funds allocated to peace-keeping operations as part of the overall allocation for foreign operations. For the Spokesman, such a measure would increase clarity and help assess the French contribution to world peace and humanitarian action.[6] At present, it is very difficult to gauge the proportion allocated to peace-keeping operations as such with any precision from the information provided to Parliament and debated by it. This is, without doubt, a most regrettable gap in the presentation of the budget.

3 France's financial relations with the United Nations

This aspect of the problem is of greater interest to the Foreign Affairs Ministry than to Defence.

The financial dispute between France and the United Nations in the 1960s

In the past, French relations with the United Nations over funding for peace-keeping operations were conflictual, during the first financial crisis of the United Nations in the mid-1960s, for example, when France refused to participate in the financing of certain United Nations operations on the basis that they were unconstitutional (see chapter 1, pp. 14 and 15). France's position on the financing of peace-keeping operations was clarified before the Committee of 33. Basically, it considered that it is up to the Security Council to determine the means of financing operations, either distributed on a sliding scale amongst all members or on the basis of voluntary contributions. The French permanent representative suggested the creation of a subsidiary organ to aid the Security Council in this task.[7]

The French position was quite close to that of the USSR, which also considered that the Security Council was the appropriate body to make such decisions. Thus the political preeminence of the Security Council was reinforced by the confirmation of its financial power by these States. On the contrary, for these States, any rupture of this parallelism through the transfer of power to the General Assembly outside the letter of the Charter also required that the financial contribution be on a voluntary basis. As this question went to the heart of the financial crisis, vivid opposition was felt, even against the advisory opinion of the International Court of Justice, to which the USSR refused to concede any legal value. Consequently, a large number of contradictory proposals were made on the question before the Committee of 33, recommending the strengthening of the powers and recovery procedures, sometimes of the General Assembly, sometimes of the Security Council.

United Nations University Press
53-70, Jingumae 5-chome
Shibuya-ku, Tokyo 150-8925
Japan

Reader's Reply Card

United Nations Peace-keeping Operations:
A Guide to French Policies
Edited by Brigitte Stern
UNUP-1009   ISBN 92-1-1009-X

Name

Address

Country

How did you come to know about this book?
☐ UNU Press Publications Catalogue
☐ Advertisement in ....
☐ Distributor ....
☐ Bookstore ....
☐ Other ....

The information on this card will help us to improve our publishing programme. Please complete the card and return it to the United Nations University Press.

What are your areas of interest?
Development ....
Social Sciences ....
Natural Resources ....
Economics ....
Food and Nutrition ....
Energy ....
International Law ....
Politics ....
Culture ....
Science and Technology ....
Other ....
☐☐☐☐☐☐☐☐☐☐☐

☐ I am interested in information about the UNU

☐ Please add my name to the catalogue mailing list ....

While France was delighted by the final decision not to apply Article 19 of the Charter to the peace-keeping operations in the Middle East and the Congo,[8] its attitude to the question was aimed at firmly defending Security Council powers. At the height of the crisis, France had equally specified clearly that it did not wish to make any promises concerning a voluntary contribution towards ending the financial difficulties of the Organization, considering that this question should be resolved globally, over and above the events in the Middle East and the Congo. There was a certain logic in this approach, which bore out France's fairly accurate predictions regarding the likely development of such operations in the future, as well as their cost. When one observes the situation of the last few years, Roger Seydoux, who was the French permanent representative to the United Nations in the 1960s, seems to have been a clairvoyant.

For many years, as a result, France turned a deaf ear to the reasoning of the Court in its 1962 advice "accepted" by the General Assembly in its Resolution 1854 A (XVIII), 19 December 1962. From 1964 on, however, the creation of peace-keeping operations was no longer decided by the General Assembly but again by the Security Council, and the Council also determined the funding methods. From then on, the situation fell into line with the French approach and France accepted the means decided upon. In fact, it discretely resolved the financial disagreement by paying its arrears in the form of voluntary contributions (commencing in 1972), without going back on its position regarding the operations in the Suez and the Congo.[9] This disagreement over funding is now ancient history.

France's current large financial contribution to PKOs

Today France pays its contribution regularly, within the required time limits – generally within the month following the appeal for funds – thus appearing a "model contributor," a circumstance often referred to by the Secretary-General of the United Nations. When he was Minister of Foreign Affairs, Alain Juppé declared before Parliament that

> if anything is unusual, it is that France fulfils its obligations in this domain with perfect regularity. I emphasize this point in so far as the French example is very rarely followed by the other large contributors. It is for this reason that we propose that the Organization adopt measures permitting it to sanction bad payers."[10]

The French share of the peace-keeping operations budget is a greater proportion than its contribution to the ordinary budget: 7.62 per cent. This is the result
of permanent membership of the Security Council, the percentage having been
set in 1973 at time when permanent members did not provide contingents to
peace-keeping operations. Times have changed and, on the contrary, countries
like France must now add the extra costs of upkeep of contingents participating
in peace-keeping operations to their already higher contributions. While these
additional costs are reimbursable, as we shall see, payment is slow in coming and
then only partial.[11] This situation explains why France is particularly attentive to
budgetary questions, which it did not fail to raise in its *aide-mémoire* in response
to *An Agenda for Peace*. There, the Minister of Foreign Affairs sets out his desire
to conserve the present system requiring a budget for each operation, which is a
guarantee of transparency and allows individual follow-up by Member States. He
also considers that the system of compulsory contributions must be maintained
(voluntary contributions being limited to States benefiting from the operation, in
so far as they have the means to do so), and comes out in favour of a detailed
cost evaluation before launching operations and the development of ongoing
audits of continuing operations.

If the cost is high, justifying close attention, France is also well aware of the
political mileage it can make from the situation. The stands taken by MPs during
debate on the finance law are revealing. True, the costs are high, but through
its massive participation in peace-keeping operations, France is "faithful to its
historic vocation, faithful to the principle of protecting peace through national
independence inspired by General de Gaulle."[12] France equally fulfils its obligations as permanent member of the Security Council[13] and serves "manifest,
vital and strategic interests, and its great power status."[14] In this way France also
upholds the law.[15]

For all of these reasons which allow it to "maintain its rank," France has
developed its participation to the point of being one of the primary troop-contributing countries for peace-keeping operations, sometimes even the largest
of all.[16] Besides, as Mr J.-F. Deniau recalled, "France is on the front line of
peace-keeping and humanitarian action. The number of our troops killed or
wounded since the beginning of the year is the cruel witness."[17]

This policy has a cost, not only human, but financial as well, which has led to
an increase in spending by the Defence Ministry.

4   The current state of France's contributions to the UN peace-keeping operations budget

The above information shows that two cases must be distinguished. The first concerns the Ministry of Foreign Affairs and relates to the "cost" of peace-keeping operations. The second, concerning the Defence Ministry, relates to "additional costs."

The financial contribution of the Ministry of Foreign Affairs

As regards the Ministry of Foreign Affairs, decision-making power is outwith French control, as it must assume its part of the "cost" of peace-keeping represented by the compulsory contribution established by the United Nations. Naturally, this varies with the total amount of funds required for peace-keeping operations during each United Nations biennial financial period. As the French Minister of Foreign Affairs noted before the vote on the 1996 Finance Bill, this amount has increased considerably, because "peace-keeping operations are becoming more and more costly. The funds allocated to them in the UN budget have gone from US\$ 482 million in 1991 to US\$ 3,2 billion in 1995,"[18] an eightfold increase. France can do little faced with Security Council decisions to set up peace-keeping operations, whether or not it participates, other than attempt to obtain a reduction of its share (something every other State wants as well) or to put pressure on all States to bring their payments up-to-date rather than leave France to be one of the few "good payers."

The financial contribution of the Ministry of Defence

On the other hand, the Defence Ministry is more concerned about a further element of the financial cost of peace-keeping operations, referred to as "additional costs." These are the real expenses of French participation in peace-keeping operations. As we have seen, they have become greater and greater as France has come to take a major place among contributing countries. France is obliged to bear the costs of its own participation, subject to later reimbursement. These expenses are hard to control. The additional costs are great and the initial budget of the Defence Ministry must be increased every year by amounts varying with technical requirements and the evolution of the international situation. Accordingly, the increase amounted to 47 per cent from 1993 to 1994, whereas the projected increase in the initial budget of 2.6 per cent for 1994–95 was totally contradicted by the 50 per cent increase which had to be accorded by a rectifying finance law on 4 August 1995.

The question of the reimbursement by the United Nations of "additional costs" incurred by States such as France is rather delicate. On average, the sums are repaid five or six years late. In addition, payments are based on a United Nations scale for the "average cost" of a soldier, whereas, in reality, for technical reasons, this cost varies widely from country to country. Consequently, the average scale for the cost of soldiers from Third World countries falls far short of covering the real cost of soldiers from industrialized countries. In the end, after six years, France receives around 25 per cent of its initial expenses, which corresponds to only 10 per cent in real terms.[19] This situation is, of course, brought up regularly in Parliament. The Minister of Foreign Affairs briefed Parliament during debate on the 1996 finance law, pointing out that the debt to France amounted to nearly a billion French francs [US$ 200 million]. He added that

> Naturally, we cannot deduct this sum from our compulsory contribution to the United Nations because we respect international laws and rules. This does show, however, that French funding for peace-keeping operations mirrors its involvement. The Finance Bill does not take account of this situation because, in practice, repayment is always made after the fact. Just as the Defence Ministry does not allocate a specific contingent for participation in future, as yet unknown operations, we do not set aside funds for potential peace-keeping operations. Everything is done later, despite the inconvenience this causes for the Budget.[20]

It should be noted, however, that there seems to be a certain amount of approximation concerning the evaluation of the UN debt. Just a year earlier, the spokesman for the Commission on Finance had set the debt at 6 billion Francs (US$ 1.2 billion), without there having been any indication that the United Nations had managed to repay the other 5 billion francs which would have allowed the Minister of Foreign Affairs to put forward the above-mentioned amount!

Whatever the real sum involved, the most important thing is that France is eventually going to have to make a hard choice. "Maintaining its rank" is praiseworthy, until the financial constraints become too great in the present context of economic difficulties. One cannot but applaud the fact that French policy has not, unlike that of some countries, contributed to the growing financial crisis within the United Nations. One must approve of the strong French involvement in UN peace-keeping operations and humanitarian action, despite its cost. On the other hand, this has led directly to a 60 per cent reduction in France's voluntary contributions to the specialized institutions and agencies of the United Nations.

Notes

1. The French Constitution of 4 October 1958 (Art. 47) and an Ordinance of 2 January 1959 with respect to finance laws specify the conditions, timing of the vote on the finance law, rectifying finance laws, and the regulatory law.
2. Trucy, "Participation de la France aux opérations de maintien de la paix," p. 145.
3. *Ibid.*
4. *Ibid.*
5. National Assembly, session of 9 November 1993, *J.O. déb. AN* 9 November 1993, p. 5673.
6. *Ibid.* p. 5678.
7. It may be noted in passing that France rejected a proposal that a permanent member of the Security Council could be exempted from payment of its contribution to a peacekeeping operation if it had abstained on the vote creating it. France considered that, once the method of financing the operation had been decided by the Security Council, it would be inconceivable for the permanent members to have such an advantage. See doc. A/5916 Annex No. 21 (A/AC.121/SR.7 at para. 14).
8. *Ibid.* See also p. 14 above.
9. On this question see C. Schricke, "L'article 17, para. 1 et 2," in J.P. Cot and A. Pellet, *La Charte des Nations Unies, Commentaire article par article* [The UN Charter: an article-by-article commentary] (Paris: Economica, 1991), pp. 355–72.
10. National Assembly session of 3 November 1994 (Debate on the 1995 finance law), *J.O. déb. AN* 3 November 1994, p. 6432.
11. See Trucy, "Participation de la France aux opérations de maintien de la paix," p. 125.
12. R. Nungesser, Spokesman for the Committee on Foreign Affairs, session of 2 November 1994 (debate on the 1995 finance law), *J.O. déb. AN* 1994, p. 6314.
13. Statement by the Minister of State and Defence Minister during the National Assembly session of 2 November 1994 before the vote on the 1995 finance law, *J.O. déb. AN* 2 November 1994, p. 6306, and during the session of 8 November 1995 before the vote on the 1996 finance law, *J.O. déb. AN* 8 November 1995, p. 3243.

14. R. Nungesser, Spokesman for the Committee on Foreign Affairs, session of 8 November 1995 (debate on the 1996 finance law), *J.O. déb. AN* 8 November 1995, p. 3218.

15. This expression was first used by President François Mitterrand with respect to the Gulf War, then was taken up before the National Assembly by the spokesman for the Committee on Foreign Affairs at the session of 8 November 1990, *J.O. déb. AN* 8 November 1990, p. 4960.

16. Declaration by the Defence Minister during a session of the National Assembly on 8 November 1995, before the vote on the 1996 finance law: "For the last few years, our country has been the primary contributor – I repeat, the primary contributor – to peace-keeping operations."

17. National Assembly session of 3 November 1992 (debate on the 1993 finance law), *J.O. déb. AN* 3 November 1992, p. 4710.

18. National Assembly session of 12 September 1995, *J.O. déb. AN* 12 September 1995, p. 3436.

19. See J.-P. Lafon in *Actualités des conflits internationaux* [Update on international conflicts] (Paris: Pédone, 1993), p. 75.

20. National Assembly session of 12 November 1995, *J.O. déb. AN* 12 November 1995, p. 3463.

4

THE MILITARY ASPECTS OF
FIELD OPERATIONS

Philippe Morillon

Innumerable foreign operations conducted by French armies, or with French participation, have taken place since the end of the Second World War and the creation of the United Nations Organization (see Appendix I, drawn up by the Ministry of Defence).

It is not surprising that, while most of the operations conducted by France up to 1990 were undertaken with a view to restoring or maintaining peace, very few were conducted under the aegis of the United Nations. From 1990 on, after the collapse of the Soviet bloc, as a permanent member of the Security Council and openly in favour of the right of humanitarian intervention for the genesis of the concept and the debate it aroused), France began to take an increasingly important place within forces deployed under the blue beret or helmet.

The evolution of peace-keeping operations and the examination of their success and failure have led to reflection on the preconditions for their creation and implementation. After an analysis of the major interventions conducted until now, the forces provided and doctrines applied, this section will draw the lessons for adapting the military apparatus presently at the Secretary-General's disposition for the conduct of United Nations missions.

I have no hesitation in repeating the belief I have been proclaiming ever since

I first took up responsibilities within the frameworks of the United Nations, as commander of UNPROFOR in Bosnia and Herzegovina, and French national forces, as a rapid-reaction force unit commander: if preventive diplomacy leads to the deployment of armed forces in a framework differing appreciably from that of traditional "interposition" peace-keeping operations, their rules of engagement must be profoundly modified by strengthening the means placed at the disposal of the commanders of the troops called upon to intervene.

To be of any use in the types of conflict in which our forces have been involved, whether in Cambodia, former Yugoslavia, Somalia, or Rwanda, we must be respected. To be respected, we must be strong.

I French military participation in major UN peace-keeping missions

Before 1991

Participation in UNTSO

France joined the operation for the supervision of the truce in the Middle East, set up after the first Arab–Israeli war, as early as June 1948. Then, as now, its contribution consisted of providing a couple of dozen observers, officers, and non-commissioned officers (NCOs), who were responsible, by their mere presence, for maintaining the still-fragile cease-fire between the belligerent parties.

These observers play a mediation and arbitration role designed to stop incidents more or less deliberately provoked by either side from degenerating into confrontations liable to blaze up into another generalized conflagration. As arbitrators, their permanent watch over a number of well-chosen observation posts allows them to discern the origins of each incident and apportion the blame among leaders at all levels by denouncing provocation and providing supporting evidence.

As mediators, they help those parties to the conflict who are not yet prepared (or resolved) to communicate other than by arms, to come to an agreement. In practical terms, this often means setting up communication networks, "hotlines" permitting immediate intervention in any serious incident through direct contact between those responsible in the field. This is essential as, right from the start, "the spiral of extreme violence" (to quote Clausewitz) arising from the vicious circle of action and reaction, must be broken. Our observers are thus "inspectors," but, to be effective, their mediation must not be limited to such simple control, which is, in reality, an acknowledgement (albeit temporary) of the failure of the ongoing peace process.

To contribute to the development of this process, they must help the combatants to prevent incidents. To this end, they must build up as many relations of trust as possible on both sides. They must make an impartial effort to understand all viewpoints. They must be prepared for this role before deployment through the study of local culture and history. Ideally, they should have some notions of Arab and Hebrew languages. Whether one likes it or not, the use of English, the working language, is indispensable.

To accomplish these missions observers do not have to be armed, as, to quote Brian Urquhart, these are non-military tasks entrusted to soldiers. Finally, they must understand that the impartiality required of them signifies neither neutrality nor passivity. They will only be effective if they can find the courage to denounce all acts, regardless of their origin, liable to harm either the most fundamental rights (which is elementary), or the simple chance of peace for which they are working.

Their job is not an easy one, for they are caught up in internecine conflict – 'between the tree and the bark' (*entre l'arbre et l'écorce*), to quote a French traditional saying advising people not to get involved in such situations. Their impartiality forbids them to make enemies, whereas, in war, as long as the cycle of violence and fear continues, only "my enemy's enemy is my friend." It must be made clear that, being nobody's enemy, our observers are condemned to being seen as obstacles, at least, if not adversaries, by all the different parties.

Participation in UNIFIL

It was from March 1978 on, as part of the United Nations Interim Force in Lebanon (UNIFIL), that French troops had their first experience of participation in the interposition missions which have led the United Nations to pass from sending unarmed observers to the deployment of combat units in (more or less temporarily suspended) conflict zones, to apply cease-fire agreements.

At the time, the idea was to establish genuine buffer zones held by international forces in particularly tense areas on the front lines, access being limited or, if possible, forbidden to the opposing forces. This can only be done with the agreement in principle of political and military leaders (which is always easy) and, in practice, agreement on zone demarcation and control techniques (which a never-ending stream of problems).

The French army has maintained a logistical support contingent of 530 men in Lebanon from 1986 until the present. At first, it also provided an infantry battalion and command structures totalling 1,380 men. Over the last eighteen years, more than 15,000 French officers, NCOs and soldiers have followed each other for tours of six months to a year in the area. In the accomplishment of this mission, they have been faced with the same difficulties as those confronting observers in UNTSO, for the above-mentioned reasons. In addition, they face problems inherent in the execution of their specific military mission of holding a buffer zone.

These difficulties result from numerous impediments to their freedom of movement and action as well as the feeble means placed at their disposal for the exercise of their right (and duty) to defend themselves. Simply resupplying a large and widespread military contingent requires the almost daily transport of tonnes of assorted stores. The resulting convoys may arouse both the desire of the belligerent parties to get hold of the stores and the fear that they will fall into the hands of their adversaries. The problem becomes even more acute once convoys start carrying humanitarian aid, as was the case in Somalia and former Yugoslavia.

In any case, the will of small local leaders to control the movements of United Nations forces despite official agreements has led to many incidents. The most serious took place, right at the beginning of the operation, when an infantry battalion commander, Col. Jean Salvan, was seriously wounded by militiamen when negotiating the free passage of his forces. But for the discipline of his battle-hardened troops, the drama could have degenerated into a catastrophe.

The desire of the United Nations to avoid the accidental involvement of its forces in the conflict they are supposed to be containing and ending is understandable. Even so, this must not be obtained at any expense, especially that of the mission itself. The doctrine for the use of UN forces, formulated in the early days of the United Nations and confirmed by the unfortunate example of its catastrophic involvement in the Congo conflict in the mid-1960s, is now unrealistic. It assumes that agreements, once reached, will be honoured, thus depriving UN forces of any effective means of retaliation if this turns out not to be the case.

The doctrine limits the use of armed force (opening fire) to narrowly defined cases of self-defence. All too often, this condemns UN soldiers to stand by, furious, without being able to intervene to put an end to flagrant, massive, and organized violations of the agreements. Even worse, it leads the public to think of them as accomplices. What use are these soldiers if they are not given the legal and material means of imposing respect for their mission, at the price of their lives if need be? It was not until the Bosnian drama and the fall of Srebrenica that it became clear that the need to protect one's own soldiers cannot be the sole reason for the deployment of armed military units.

In the meantime, 15 French soldiers serving with UNIFIL have given their lives since 1978 and 42 have been wounded (see Appendix II). Although the cease-fire has been violated many times, peace will come eventually and their sacrifices will not have been vain.

Post–Cold War engagements

Participation in UNTAC

France's agreement, in March 1991, to make a strong contribution to the military component of the United Nations Transitional Authority in Cambodia (UNTAC) marks its engagement to take an increasing part in peace-keeping operations under United Nations authority. This turnaround stemmed from the desire of the French President and Government to play a part commensurate with permanent member status in the development of the military mechanism placed at the UN Secretary-General's disposal for the implementation of his *Agenda for Peace*.

With the collapse of the Soviet regime came the end of the systematic Soviet veto of any operation which might involve the slightest intervention in the internal affairs of Member States. At the same time, numerous crises broke out around the world, especially in regions which had been subject to the influence of the USSR (and 40 years of more or less brutal reign of the "Pax Sovietica") until then. The first of these serious crises occurred in Cambodia, followed quickly by the mushrooming of civil wars of varying degrees of severity in Croatia, Somalia, Bosnia and Herzegovina, and finally Rwanda.

In Cambodia, 115 French officers and NCOs participated in the United Nations Advance Mission in Cambodia, UNAMIC, from November 1991. They were reinforced after June 1992 by the French contingent of UNTAC, made up of 1,500 men under the authority of a brigadier–general, second in command to the commanding officer of the military component of UNTAC. The two missions together lasted 24 months, until November 1993, after the successful organization of elections throughout the country at the end of May 1993. A total of 6,400 French soldiers took part in these operations, with tours of duty averaging six months.

In this country, destroyed by nearly 20 years of civil war, the ambition of the signatories to the peace agreements was to allow national reconciliation through elections held under United Nations control in an atmosphere of confidence obtained by the disarmament and demobilization of the factions. At the same time, one of the keys to saving Cambodia was to be its economic rehabilitation, helping the rural areas to overcome their backwardness and assisting in their development.

From 1 October 1992 to 3 June 1993, the most important period of the mission, Brigadier-General Robert Rideau was the French officer second in command to the military component's commanding officer. The following analysis is an extract from the report he wrote for the French Armed Forces Chief of Staff upon his return. Of course, all confidential information has been removed.

Apart from the success of the elections, it must be acknowledged that the assessment of UNTAC against the objectives it pursued is less black and white. In this case, the good and the mediocre run side by side.

Among the positive points, a special mention must be given to the Office of the UN High Commissioner for Refugees (UNHCR), which managed to find judicious alternative solutions to a plan which was initially too rigid, inappropriate to the aspirations and mentalities of the 350,000 refugees. From then on, it was able to close the seven camps implanted in Thailand progressively and repatriate the occupants to the region of their choice. Thus, even the 77,000 of them from camps controlled by the Khmer Rouge regained their liberty.

The work of the civil administration also merits a mention, even though it was never able to exercise fully its mandate for control over all of the existing administrative structures. Prevented from acting as it hoped by the refusal of Pol Pot's forces to allow free access to their zones, it was forced to limit its action essentially to control over the "State of Cambodia." While this objective might seem modest, in reality it covered 90 per cent of Cambodia and the only existing administrative system. The dogged work of the component thwarted the pressure exerted on electors by government forces. FUNCINPEC's victory at the general election in May 1993 is further proof (if any is needed) of the effectiveness of this control, which included real technical assistance initiatives. In particular, the adoption of provisions concerning the judicial system and freedom of movement were significant breakthroughs.

The assessment of the military component is more equivocal. Demining training eventually reached a satisfactory rhythm despite a chaotic beginning due to inadequate funding. The objectives set were met and coherent mechanisms were set up. It may thus be hoped that the pharaonic task remaining to clean up Cambodia will proceed under acceptable conditions. Of course, this will be a long-winded process, estimated at ten years, but a necessary one if the list of victims is not to grow indefinitely and much excellent farmland left uncultivated.

On the other hand, the essential mission of disarming and demobilizing the factions was a failure. Only 50,000 men left the armed forces after handing in their weapons (generally in very bad condition) to United Nations forces. If this did not significantly perturb the electoral process, it is a cause for concern for the still uncertain future.

As for the rehabilitation of the country, it remained embryonic due to lack of funds (only 20 per cent of the US$ 880 million promised were released) and lack of organization.

The main cause of dysfunction in the heavy-handed UNTAC set-up was the set-up itself. Its "comb" structure, placing all the components on the same level, would have been indisputable if the Secretary-General's special representative had had a cabinet director (or chief of staff) responsible for coordination of the whole system. This is not the case, with the result that each department works within its own area of responsibility while almost totally ignoring the work of the others. In this respect, it should be noted that the force commander's position is ambiguous. Theoretically second in command of the operation, he is, in fact, placed on the same level as the other component directors. As with the other directors, he has not received the slightest financial allocation to implement his mandate. In this respect he is subject to the good will of the administrative director, who has power to decide on the validity of all requests for money, even those dictated by operational imperatives.

Finally, the absence of any real internal information policy reduces the effectiveness of the ensemble by giving a free hand to the wildest of rumours, obligingly repeated by an omnipresent international press longing for incidents. In this way, the reinforcement of security measures decided upon a few weeks before the elections, fully justified but badly explained, gave credit to the belief that the Khmer Rouge planned serious disruption of the elections. Fortunately, the optimism displayed by a number of leaders helped calm people, allowing them to regain their lost confidence.

The mission of the military component, initially centred on disarming and demobilizing the factions, evolved during the operation in response to events. Indeed, as early as October 1992, there was no longer the slightest doubt that this objective was unattainable when the Khmer Rouge refused to open up the zones under its control. It was not just that Pol Pot's forces did not disarm, but that in so doing they gave the other factions (especially the State of Cambodia) an argument for no longer proceeding with a process which would thus have modified the existing balance of forces.

This situation, unforeseen in the Paris Peace Agreements, logically resulted in the increased participation of the military component in securing the overall election process. This mission was implicitly approved in February 1993 by Security Council Resolution 792. Indeed, it then appeared clearly that, in a country in a state of latent civil war, swarming with arms, the civil components of UNTAC, if left to themselves, would be incapable of keeping the peace and establishing a climate conducive to the holding of a general election. Consequently, the military component took entire responsibility for the co-ordination of operations during the five-week electoral campaign and the week of voting, at the district, provincial, and Phnom Penh command levels. In addition, the excessive number of polling stations, initially set arbitrarily by technocrats at 1,800, was reduced to 1,500, showing a realism missing until then.

Respect for the UN forces fell rapidly throughout the mission. The reasons may be found in the difficulty they had in maintaining strictly impartial behaviour and in convincing the factions of the validity of such an approach. In a peace-keeping operation there is no designated adversary, there are only reprehensible acts (the Security Council never excluded the Khmer Rouge from the peace process). As a result, resentment crystallized against the Blue Helmets, who were accused alternatively of doing too much and not enough. Such changes of situation should be taken into account from the start, in order to anticipate acts liable to put the security of personnel at risk.

Mission support is the UN's responsibility. Now, for structural reasons, response time proved to be particularly long (in Cambodia, a number of months passed before the basic organization was in place; supplementary civilian helicopters for the election period never arrived). For this reason, the proposal being studied at present for the constitution of a stock of immediately available logistical support allowing the equipment of our forces with indispensable campaign provisions, seems most judicious. It goes without saying that these "extra-national contributions" must be retrieved as soon as the UN is able to take over.

The two official languages of the UN are French and English. Though it may displease dyed-in-the-wool French-speakers, knowledge of the English language is indispensable for efficient day-to-day work in multinational operations. Fundamental questions must also, however, be dealt with in French, whether orally or written, so as to avoid any ambiguity. It should be noted that the majority of high-ranking UN officials master our language perfectly.

As organized at present, the staff of the military components is unable to conduct peace-keeping operations with the required efficiency. Structural reform will be needed to remedy this, perhaps involving the creation of regional military staffs (Europe, Asia, America, Africa). While still based on the intangible multinational principle, they would have the specific vocation of following the evolution of regional crises, implementing common training procedures and, if necessary, preparing interventions decided upon by the Security Council and providing the *skeleton* of the military staff of forces deployed.

General Rideau's conclusions agree with some of those stressed in my analysis of the interventions in the Middle East and Lebanon. They will be taken up after the study of the operations in the former Yugoslavia, Somalia, and Rwanda.

Participation in UNPROFOR in Croatia

In application of the Vance Plan, once it was accepted by Belgrade and Zagreb in January 1992, the Security Council decided to deploy a United Nations interposition force on all Croatian territory occupied by the Yugoslavian federal army after the revolt by the Serb majority population of Krajina and Slavonia against Croatian national authority. The force's mission involved verifying the withdrawal of the federal army, ensuring the demilitarization of the protected areas, protecting the local population, and aiding the return of refugees pending the achievement of an overall political solution to the status of the territories. Hence the title: United Nations Protection Force (UNPROFOR).

Reuniting contingents and personnel from Vancouver to Vladivostok and from Moscow to Buenos Aires, the force was deployed progressively from April 1992 in four sectors representing the four United Nations Protected Areas (UNPA) in northern and southern Krajina and western and eastern Slavonia. The military headquarters was set up in Sarajevo in March, under Indian Lt.-Gen. Satish Nambiar. Two logistical bases were chosen in Belgrade and Zagreb. Along with command components, France provided an infantry battalion and a logistics battalion group. France being the largest contributing country, a French major-general was named second in command of the operation.

Despite a very good initial welcome, the battalions were quickly confronted by the problems already experienced in the Middle East and Cambodia. In addition, new problems arose immediately, mainly related to the extremely long period between the signature of the agreements and their coming into force, but also due to the insubordination of local Serb leaders.

When the Vance Plan was accepted, the limits of the various protected areas were drawn up with regard to both local administrative boundaries (*obstine* in Serbo-Croatian) and the situation in the field. During the three-month period needed to set up, train, and deploy the first contingents of the international force (the furthest afield took six months to reach their stations), the front lines had changed, generally in favour of the Serbs. The Serbs energetically resisted giving up even an inch of such "liberated" territory, even when it involved previously Croatian majority areas. Belgrade supported this position taken by the leaders of the "self-proclaimed Serb Republic of Krajina."

It would take months of interminable negotiations and successive violations of the cease-fire before a solution was found. This involved creating "pink zones" around the UNPAs, incorporating the contested areas, from which the Serbs were to withdraw, but which the Croatian army was forbidden to enter. Despite joint supervision by the United Nations and the European Community Monitoring Mission, these zones continued to be the scene of most serious incidents.

In the implementation of the other, less contested agreements, UN representatives came up against another, practically insurmountable form of opposition from local Serb political chiefs. Among these leaders, the extremists used terror tactics to impose their hegemony over the more reasonable leaders. They simply refused to consider themselves bound by agreements signed in Belgrade and Zagreb, loudly demanding independence. They impudently claimed the implementation of those agreements going in their favour while rejecting the rest – "Everything I have is mine, the rest is negotiable." Consequently, the repatriation of refugees was never feasible as long as they were in power. This was to become the major (justified) grievance of the Croatian Government and people during the 40 months between the arrival of UNPROFOR and the successful Croatian surprise attack in August 1995.

In addition to these two major internal problems – unsuitable agreements and local refusal to apply them – the outbreak of hostilities in Bosnia and Herzegovina represented a third source of difficulty right from the start of the mission. As stated above, Sarajevo was chosen as the military headquarters of the operation. This was done for two eminently political reasons. Firstly, by not choosing Belgrade or Zagreb, the chances of becoming hostage to one of the parties to the conflict were reduced. Secondly, it was hoped that the presence of Blue Helmets in Sarajevo would help prevent the outbreak of the major crisis then brewing in Bosnia.

When the crisis came, the military staff and commander were no longer able to exercise their responsibilities. Eventually, in mid-May, Lieutenant-General Nambiar was forced to transfer his headquarters, first to Belgrade and then to Zagreb. As a result, during the first two crucial months, as the mission was starting up, the Commander-in-Chief's authority had great difficulty in making itself felt in the field.

In the end, apart from western Slavonia, Croatia's problems were all resolved by Croatian armed force. Should this be seen as the total failure of the United Nations?

I sincerely believe not. During its 40 months in Croatia, UNPROFOR's contingents contributed to the fairly constant maintenance of the cease-fire, at least. On the night of the arrival in Belgrade of UNPROFOR's military command from New York, 8 March 1992, the Slavonic town of Osijek was hit by 300 shells. Four months later, in July 1992, the local farmers started working the land on each side of the front lines. In the following years of UN presence, apart from rare Croatian offensives, violations of the cease-fire were limited to skirmishes.

Even so, these results cannot be glorified. The lessons from this affair, and all the others, must be retained.

Participation in UNPROFOR in Bosnia and Herzegovina

The situation in Bosnia and Herzegovina deteriorated rapidly after its recognition by the European Community on 6 April 1992, leading to generalized anarchy. We have seen how this catastrophic situation (the term "Lebanon-ization" was coined, whereas in Lebanon one spoke of Balkanization) forced the headquarters of UNPROFOR to leave Sarajevo in mid-May, leaving behind only a company of 150 French soldiers under the command of an Australian, Col. John Wilson.

UNHCR specialists and their counterparts in humanitarian NGOs immediately became alarmed by the likely consequences of this situation. After having been driven from their land by intimidation and massacres, hundreds of thousands of displaced persons had gathered in the north-western Bihac pocket, the Travnik–Vitez region of central Bosnia, and the Tuzla region in the east. Also, 300,000 inhabitants were under siege in Sarajevo. The experts estimated that, in these conditions, at least 1,500,000 people were unlikely to survive the winter.

At this time, sometimes exaggerated revelations began to appear of atrocities committed in camps: rape, murder, the destruction of vital installations, and extortion committed by groups heeding neither government nor law. Public opinion was moved and the pressure mounted at UN headquarters, despite the near-exhaustion of its military and financial resources.

After the London Conference, UNPROFOR was ordered to hold Sarajevo airport, under Serb control, to allow an airlift to be set up. For this purpose, a Canadian infantry battalion taken from the forces deployed in Croatia was sent to reinforce the soldiers remaining in Sarajevo. The Canadian major-general, Lewis MacKenzie, until then Chief of Staff, took command of one sector of Sarajevo, where his forces were joined by three supplementary infantry battalions, one each from Egypt, the Ukraine, and France. The airport was opened on 29 June 1992 after the audacious visit by French President François Mitterrand, who had landed the previous evening under machine-gun fire. It soon became clear, however, that this effort would not suffice. Road corridors would also have to be opened from Belgrade and the Adriatic Coast to allow the delivery of enough supplies for the survival of the inhabitants of the various urban enclaves spread throughout Bosnia.

The concept of a humanitarian operation was decided upon for want of any military intervention, the latter having been excluded by the Security Council. Even before receiving any official mandate, UNPROFOR began studying the form this might take, in conjunction with the UNHCR special representative in Zagreb, the Spaniard José-Maria Mendeluce. Military staff studies showed that at least four infantry battalions would be needed, initially to be stationed in the Bihac pocket, Tuzla, Mostar, and at Banja Luka in the Serb-controlled part of central Bosnia.

New York managed to obtain engagements from France, the United Kingdom,

Canada, and Spain to provide one infantry battalion group each, at their own cost. Holland and Belgium formed a joint transport battalion, the Danes provided headquarters components, the French joined the English in offering a combined light airborne army unit, and the French placed an engineering battalion at the disposal of the new force.

As this action was sure to have repercussions on the forces already deployed in Croatia, it was decided to place the new force under the overall command of UNPROFOR in Zagreb, with a major-general in direct command and with his command post in Bosnia and Herzegovina. This became known as BH Command. Having been designated to the command, I gathered the civil and military representatives of the contributing nations in Zagreb in mid-September for a week of discussions on organization of the command, deployment of the forces, and the mission itself. Mendeluce and his staff participated because UNHCR had been designated lead agency for the operation.

A great advantage in getting the operation off the ground was the decision to form the core of the command staff out of the existing NATO Northag staff, the announced dissolution of which had made it immediately available. In this way, more than a third of the command post staff already knew each other and had worked well together. This gave immediate cohesion and remarkable efficiency to the whole staff and, with few exceptions, most of the external components had no trouble fitting in.

The first operational orders were thus able to be sent out to the battalions before they left their home barracks. Careful account was taken of the existing United Nations rules of engagement in writing these orders, their spirit being clarified and adapted to the terms of the special mandate of the mission. This involved ensuring the delivery of humanitarian assistance, mediating between the factions with a view to bringing them to the negotiating table, and laying the military groundwork for the application of the peace plan being negotiated in Geneva. Basically, the battalions would try to save as many human lives as possible and alleviate suffering amongst the population. This might be summarized as the duty to assist persons in danger. The rules regarding the use of force were copied from those in force in Croatia: retaliation authorized in self-defence.

As soon as it arrived, the staff of BH Command was confronted with the danger of an imminent Serb attack aimed at cutting Sarajevo in two, the better to take it completely. The following paragraphs are written in the first person to show the extent to which I was forced, despite my best efforts, to play a political role right from the start of the mission.

I immediately set off for Pale to meet Karadzic, the leader of the Bosnian Serbs, and his entourage. I tried to convince them that a military victory in Sarajevo, whilst possible, would be infinitely costly to human life and a political and diplomatic catastrophe. I told them I was convinced that the world could not remain indifferent to such an act and that they must weigh up the risks of provoking a military intervention.

The meeting lasted for hours. They all attempted to make me understand that it was their duty to come to the aid of their brothers held hostage in Sarajevo, despised, mistreated and deprived of all humanitarian assistance. Their intention was limited to gathering these people in one part of the town, the larger part remaining under Muslim control. They wanted partition, like Beirut, like Berlin.

I drew their attention to their means of action. I told them that history would judge the Serb nation on the use they had made and continued to make of the blind force of artillery. Images of the ravaging of Vukovar and Sarajevo had led to unanimous disapproval and the imposition of sanctions. Despite what they might think, nobody wanted to put an end to the Serbs, but everyone held a grudge against them for such indiscriminate killing. They explained that their advantage in heavy armaments made up for their numerical inferiority and that they would never risk losing this strategic balance.

Throughout the meeting, I forced myself to listen with great attention and not judge them. It was my duty as a mediator. The public would have a great deal of difficulty understanding this attitude. How could one avoid taking sides against those who had, with absolute cynicism, propagated and implemented their own peculiar racist theory; avoid becoming enemies without appearing to be friends; talk to people who should be eliminated?

This is the fundamental problem. Although a military leader, I am convinced that politics must take the primary position. Politicians must determine the moment when politics can only continue through war. The resort to war is only possible when all political means have been exhausted and the use of military force has a chance of serving the political aims set by governments. The fathers of the Catholic Church teach that war can only ever be a lesser evil and that it must only be embarked upon if there is a chance of winning. To get this idea across to journalists, I have evoked the image of a surgeon who would never attempt an operation if he were sure that the patient could not survive.

What are the political goals fixed by the world in Bosnia if not to put an end to the policy of ethnic cleansing and allow the inhabitants of the country to rebuild the harmonious model which governed their relations before the crisis broke? Wouldn't taking sides for any one community today run the risk of widening the gap between them irremediably?

This is the real question and not, as has been said, that there would have been too many risks in such an operation, especially for our lightly armed Blue Helmets, always open to being taken hostage. Of course this risk existed, but we had prepared for it as was our duty. To present matters in this light runs the risk of being accused of cowardice, an accusation which the public did in fact make.

I had the advantage of believing that the hatred between these communities was not so strong that no reconciliation was possible between them. The accounts I continually received throughout the country proved this. I believe that peace is possible and that the leaders must be helped to work out the conditions. Pending a political solution, everything must be done to reduce the suffering of the population. That is the sense in which I understood my mission. That is why I volunteered for the command. That is why I will continue to pass from one side to the other, in the hope that they will come to agreement through me.

In any case, the results of this first encounter were not very convincing.

On 31 October, one day before the start of the "week of peace" requested by UNICEF, the Serbs launched their most violent offensive in weeks, perhaps since the beginning of hostilities. This would be the last serious attempt to take Sarajevo. Perhaps, after this defeat, my arguments may have helped the politicians convince the military.

The aim of this paper is not to describe all the events which followed the first contact up until the end of the mission and the relief of the Blue Helmets by IFOR on 15 December 1995 after the signature of the Dayton Agreements in Paris a day earlier. For three long years, the Blue Helmets were confronted with difficulties well known to all interposition missions, but they were deployed in the absence of any prior agreement, thus inaugurating an intermediate series of interventions, such as those in Somalia and Rwanda, where it would no longer be possible to speak of peace-keeping as such, nor of direct "peacemaking" or "peace enforcement" interventions such as those in Korea and Kuwait.

Under the direction of the Under-Secretary-General for Peace-keeping Operations and his department, the United Nations has had to build a new doctrine and the corresponding means. It was not until the shocking spectacle for world opinion of the fall of Srebrenica in July 1995 that military leaders' repeated requests for a modification of their rules of engagement relating to the use of armed force in this specific context were taken into account. The 30 August 1995 intervention by the land forces of the rapid reaction force, with air support from NATO warplanes, represented a watershed for Bosnian history, of course, but also, in my opinion, for all future interventions.

Abandoning the unworldly attitude which had condemned its troops to powerlessness (which had come to a head on Ascension weekend 1995, when the world watched its soldiers imprisoned and in chains in Serb barracks around Sarajevo), the United Nations has understood that throughout the operation the local warlords had been strong only to the extent that the United Nations were weak. By finally giving its soldiers the authority and means to retaliate, not only when their own lives were in danger, but also whenever their freedom of movement in the exercise of their mandate was obstructed, the United Nations had understood that to limit violence its military forces must be able to implement the mandate whilst throwing down the challenge, "Shoot at us, if you dare."

Once again, having said this, despite the criticism, the United Nations action in Bosnia was useful. Nobody died of hunger there, despite the justified alarm amongst specialists which had led to the operation. This zone of disorder, which ran the risk of degenerating into a generalized conflagration, was contained. Today the blaze has been put out and it may be hoped that there are no hidden embers still smouldering.

Among the 45,000 French soldiers who were deployed in the field from February 1992 to December 1995 (see Appendix II), 53 gave their lives in the accomplishment of the mission and 580 were wounded. If national opinion accepted this price without hostile reaction, it must be that, deep down, the French were aware that it was worthwhile.

I think they were right.

Participation in UNOSOM

In December 1992, a few months after the start of the humanitarian assistance operation in Bosnia, world opinion was shaken by scenes of the victims of famine in Somalia, and the Security Council decided to send a new interposition force to this country ravaged by civil war. France participated in this operation, called UNOSOM (United Nations Operation in Somalia), with a 2,050-man force responsible for a zone-control and logistics mission. The operation did enable an end to be put to the famine, but failed to resolve the political problems.

The first phase ended in May 1993, leaving the bitter after-taste of yet another defeat for the international community.

The military and technical reasons for this apparent failure are related to those already pointed out for this sort of "neither peace nor war" intervention; but also, in this case, the international forces involved in the humanitarian assistance operation found themselves caught up in a war action against Gen. Mohamed Farah Aidid's partisans, clearly intended to go beyond the exercise of their right and duty to retaliate, so as to attack and capture him. Using the civilian population as a shield, General Aidid managed to give the whole world the image of soldiers of peace shooting at women and children. This was intolerable.

Moreover, the operation showed up the limits, and perhaps the wrongness, of the "zero deaths" theory. The death of 18 American Rangers in an ambush in Mogadishu could not be accepted by the American public and led to the withdrawal of the GIs.

Every military operation involves risks. It is up to the military commander to advise the political authorities of this before any decision to engage forces is taken. Once the decision is made, the consequences must be accepted and the public prepared. If not, international forces will be at the mercy of the slightest trouble-maker in every operation. It will be enough to murder a few Blue Helmets to have their contingents pull out. To countenance such fragility would condemn peace soldiers everywhere to being taken hostage.

Operation Turquoise in Rwanda

Just a few words, to finish, on Operation Turquoise, undertaken by France in Rwanda from 23 June to 30 September 1994, with 2,000 men reinforced by African battalions, in application of Security Council Resolution 929 of 22 June 1994.

Clearly set spatial and temporal objectives, the dissuasive use of force in reply to any attempted aggression not only against UN soldiers but also against the refugees they were there to protect, avoided an even greater human catastrophe than the genocide which preceded the intervention. Deployed in the space of a few days, thanks to the use of large-capacity aerial troop transports rented from the army of the former USSR to assemble contingents already present in Africa, the French battalions carried out their operations perfectly, foreshadowing the missions given to the soldiers of the rapid reaction force in Bosnia a year later.

They set up real protected areas in the region near the Zairian border, to allow refugees fleeing the advance of the Tutsi army to regroup. In so doing they used armed force at least twice to prevent attempted incursions into the protected regions. Thanks to this rapid intervention, sanitary systems were able to be set up to stop the cholera epidemic and the NGOs were able to play their role in safety.

Current events in Burundi, from which even the Red Cross has had to pull out, show that in crises of this nature, humanitarian aid and military protection can and must continue to cooperate.

2   Lessons from recent peace-keeping operations

Informed readers will not be surprised to find that this section addresses the three aspects of traditional military analysis: leadership, mission, and means of action.

The need for a leader

The chain of command

The most urgent need is for reform of the chain of command and the relations between it and the governments and military staff of troop-contributing countries. The current faults in the system were clearly in evidence during the Somali operation and at the beginning of the operation in former Yugoslavia.

The conclusions of the Rideau report on the Cambodia operation, set out above, should be reflected upon in the search for indispensable unity of command. Finally, the conditions particular to the United Nations command set-up in Bosnia and Herzegovina indicate the right direction to follow. Efforts must be directed at improving operational planning and implementation systems.

Initial planning

Most people agree that the planning mechanism at the Secretary-General's disposal needs improvement, but, in truth, its major task should be to ensure consultations with qualified representatives of troop-contributing nations *before* any decision is made to launch a new operation or vote Security Council resolutions defining mandates. The aim of such consultation would be to obtain formal agreement from governments on the nature of and practical considerations for the proposed operation, allowing a delegation of sovereignty over the troops provided to the operational command. For want of such prior agreement, the force commander in Somalia was constantly obliged to negotiate each proposed mission for the soldiers under his command with the interested governments. To put it mildly, he had trouble exercising his command.

In September 1992, when an operation in Bosnia and Herzegovina was approved in principle, the initiative was taken, with New York's approval, to hold a reunion in Zagreb to propose and discuss command and support structures, force deployment, and rules of engagement. Due to the resulting agreement, there were few problems in the relations between the Commander-in-Chief and the various contingents. This was only possible because he had access to the resources of the existing military staff of UNPROFOR and because not many nations were involved. It would not be possible to apply this system to all operations.

It is in New York that this essential task should be undertaken. It seems that it would be worth while setting up a *specialized office, situated at Secretary-General level*, given the political implications of the decisions to be made. It should include at least 20 high-level specialists and might recruit its core membership from the Committee of Chiefs of Staff of the permanent members of the Security Council. Whenever possible, the designated intervention force commander should participate in all discussions and decisions of the office.

The conduct of operations

Any temptation towards excessive centralization of the conduct of operations in New York should be resisted. Creating a "super-Pentagon" would not suffice, as wide responsibility must be given to the force commander in the field in such situations. Even so, considerable improvements must be made to the corresponding structures at both levels.

At UN headquarters, the existing peace-keeping operations situation room, under the Secretary-General, merely follows up on operations through information provided by its forces in the field and the media. It should be given official access to intelligence obtained by the specialized agencies of the major troop-contributing countries and the means necessary to put this to good use.

At the force command level, it is no longer possible to patch together a military staff out of as wide a range of participating nations as possible and still retain operational efficiency. While preserving the principle of multinationality, the skeleton of the military staff must be built up either around one dominant nation or, preferably, out of existing international military staffs.

The proposal to set up *regional military staffs* is now accepted unanimously. General Rideau has taken it up as well. The aim of such organizations would be to follow the evolution of regional crises, set up and implement common training programmes, and, if necessary, plan envisaged operations jointly with New York. Within such organizations, emphasis should be placed on specialized intelligence offices, relations with the press, and psychological action, three areas currently neglected for various reasons.

Above all, I repeat, the need for a unified command must be taken into account. United Nations traditions have led to the creation of too many parallel hierarchies, civil affairs, administration, observers, and humanitarian assistance organizations, working separately and with little coordination.

The need for a clear mission

The distinction between peace-keeping operations set up under Chapter VI of the United Nations Charter, and Chapter VII peacemaking operations authorized to resort to veritable war action, is not as clear as it used to be. Since questions of a right or duty of intervention have arisen, United Nations interventions falling between the two above-mentioned categories have multiplied, leading inevitably to an unfortunate incompatibility.

If this right is finally recognized (which France considers necessary, although other countries are not convinced), we must learn from recent experience and realize that, in this framework, the use of armed force must be strictly limited to the exercise of the right (and duty) of self-defence, but "an enlarged concept of self-defence" such as was employed by the rapid reaction force in Bosnia and Herzegovina. In this context, soldiers of peace are exposed to widespread resentment because of their inability to take sides in conflicts and must, therefore, be equipped with the most modern means of active and passive protection. This will be dealt with below.

With respect to military intervention as such (under Chapter VII), the idea, widely held by the public and some government leaders, that war can be clinical and operations undertaken without any risk for our troops, must be dispelled. This perverse idea, born out of the Gulf War, is now dominant. It is the cause of the questions and doubts arising with respect to the attitude of the United Nations. This does not mean that soldiers of peace are condemned to remain impassive as long as the use of force is limited to self-defence. It is important to fight against the tendency in New York, inherited from decades of peace-keeping operations in which it was acceptable, to give the military non-military tasks of simply observing and reporting.

The need for appropriate means of action

This section will first look at the question of needs from the international angle of endowing the Secretary-General with a deterrent capability adapted to his determination to emphasise preventive diplomacy. It will then propose a re-orientation for doctrine, equipment, support, and training for national armed forces.

Constituting a reserve pool of forces at the Secretary-General's disposal

As long as there is no world government to give it orders, there can be no world army.

To reduce the currently prohibitive time-spans required to gather the forces necessary for his operations, the UN Secretary-General is counting on the con-stitution of a "reserve stock of forces and standard peace-keeping equipment,"[1] which the contributing countries would agree to keep at his disposal on short notice. This idea is gaining support and a good many of the nations consulted have responded favourably or should do so. The creation of a permanent rapid intervention force along these lines was one of the major points of the final report of a special committee of the United States Congress, for example.

It is clear that the contributing countries will never give up sovereignty over their armed forces without prior consultation. It is, thus, out of the question to dream of a force comparable to the French Rapid Action Force, able to intervene within 48 hours. Even so, keeping an up-to-date list of specialized units, kept on alert in their own countries pending their government's green light to intervene, would be the basis of all planning and would allow the Security Council to avoid resolving to create missions without having the means to get them off the ground. Given the delay necessary for a decision, this measure would permit a reduction of the deployment time-lag (of at least three months in the present state of affairs) to less than a month. That would already be a great improvement.

Care should be taken with respect to the proposed creation and upkeep of permanent stocks of equipment by some countries which do not provide fighting men. It would appear difficult for a government or its public to accept such costs without having the right to use the stocks for national purposes, especially as additional installations and officials would be required to train the foreign teams for whom the equipment is destined.

Equipment

Troop protection

Equipment needs must be conceived with regard to the imperative protection needs of the troops. To be able to exercise their right and duty of self-defence, the forces must have the means to put an end immediately to any attack upon them, through effective retaliation. The threats will continue to consist of direct infantry or armoured fire as well as indirect mortar or artillery fire.

First, threats must be able to be detected. To react to direct fire, armoured and turreted vehicles are necessary, preferably on wheels, as caterpillar tracks add to the deterioration of the road infrastructure. Faced with indirect fire, ground-to-ground counter-batteries must be developed using intelligent weapons. Pending their development, close air support is indispensable.

This is all active protection, the best, mainly because it gives the public the impression that the forces are not powerless. Even so, individual and collective passive protection measures should not be neglected. Specifically, the use of sand bags to prepare the terrain, whilst effective, takes too long.

The threat of mines should not be forgotten. De-mining efforts should continue, although the proper, highly-equipped specialists are still too few.

Battlefield surveillance

Peace forces must reassure by their presence and must, therefore, be armed appropriately. They must also be arbitrators. To do so they must be given the means to "catch low blows in the scrum" (i.e., to catch those who attack when the referee is not looking). The whole range of land, air, and space investigation techniques could be of use in this task, including radar, abandoned ground captors, aerial and satellite observation and the like.

Communications

Satellite transmissions are the only really safe and efficient means of long-distance communication. In the field, their use also allows permanent follow-up on convoys, which, for humanitarian assistance tasks, is essential.

For tactical communications, there is no present need for high-performance equipment. Commercially available radios such as Motorola work perfectly well.

Logistics

United Nations logistics are slow and costly. The administration in New York should realize that it is in its interest to adopt working budget procedures. Accelerated budgetary procedures are also being investigated.

In any case, delays will still remain long, with comparable effects on delivery. Pending the benefit of planned but unimplemented standardization measures, most major powers are now thinking in terms of the French initiative set aside a four to six months stock of replacement parts, rather than the two months currently required by the United Nations.

Health support must get first priority, with second-line efforts being made for MASH units.

The preparation of national armed forces

This section deals only with proposals for the preparation of operations under Chapter VI of the Charter, as Chapter VII interventions obey rules for which all armies are prepared.

Doctrine

The time has passed when soldiers of peace could – and had to – act like British policemen with whistles and no truncheons. They must be respected through deterrence and protected from deliberate aggression whenever deterrence fails.

The threat to use massive air strikes is currently the best deterrent in low- and medium-intensity conflicts, where pacification forces may be engaged. Doctrine should be based on the experience with nuclear weapons. The threat must be credible and the final decision to use force must be made at the highest political level. This is a strategy of the non-use of force; the actual use of these means would signify the end, or radical transformation, of the mission. This was the strategy used by the international community, at French instigation, to raise the siege of Sarajevo at the beginning of 1994. The situation may fail in the field if local authorities cannot control their partisans or because of resentment due to the refusal of the peace forces to take sides. The military staff must be prepared for this eventuality and the units in the field must have the greatest possible operational capability.

There cannot be two sorts of forces ready for deployment, one for peace-keeping missions and the other for war. The effectiveness shown by contingents of all sorts in recent operations would seem to prove the point. This does not mean that there is no need for pre-deployment training to impart indispensable technical know-how in observation post installation, manning check points on major axes, convoy escorting, road clearing, and so on. At the present time, all countries prepare their contingents in practically the same manner before deployment.

Training

French army training for peace-keeping operations occurs mainly during coordination camps immediately preceding departure on mission. These camps last four weeks, compared to 12 weeks for the British. The best balance is probably somewhere between the two. In fact, in every army, the transfer of know-how on an ongoing mission is essentially achieved between arriving and departing units. The designations are known early enough for a number of months to be devoted to preparing the mission.

The best-trained combat units are also the best prepared for the "neither peace nor war" situations with which they are confronted in the resolution of present (and future) crises. The most important effort for special preparation must be made at the officer and NCO level.

In peace-keeping operations, success arises out of each officer and NCO's day-to-day practice of a culture of international relations based on information, communication, and the respect for procedure. The peace soldier must add to his expert combat training the ability to use the minimum possible controlled violence and the ability to negotiate. To play a pacifying role, the officer must be prepared to understand all those with whom he deals, so as to help them to come to agreement through him. Prior to each mission, he must receive intensive training in the culture, history and, if possible, rudiments of the language of the country to which he is being sent.

Note

1.   S/1995/1, 3 January 1995, para. 45.

5

THE CIVILIAN ASPECTS OF FIELD OPERATIONS

Philippe Morillon

In addition to the military objectives traditionally entrusted to the military personnel of peace-keeping operations, such as supervising cease-fires, regrouping, and demobilizing troops, which constitute the backbone of so-called "first generation" of peace-keeping operations, a number of tasks have come to be included in the mandates of peace-keeping operations which may be described as civilian.

I The substantial development of civilian tasks

These tasks cover a particularly wide range of fields and may take place during all three of the stages of conflict resolution defined by Boutros Boutros-Ghali in *An Agenda for Peace*: peacemaking, peace-keeping and peace-building.

The following tasks may be considered civilian aspects of peace-keeping operations.[1]

• the reintegration of combatants into civilian life;
• de-mining;
• the return of refugees and displaced persons;
• the supervision of existing administrative structures;
• the establishment of new police forces;
• the verification of respect for human rights;

- the design and supervision of constitutional, judicial, and electoral reforms;
- the observation, supervision and even organization and conduct of elections;
- the coordination of support for economic rehabilitation and reconstruction.

Of course, the provision of humanitarian assistance (food, medicines, and the like) to civilian populations who are the victims of conflict must be added to this list.

Even so, it would not be correct to conclude that such missions are peculiar to the most recent peace-keeping operations which are described as "second-generation" peace-keeping operations when their mandate extends to non-military concerns. In fact, a number of "traditional" peace-keeping operations, especially the very first, undertook humanitarian aid or assistance tasks. UNIFIL's mandate, for example, included the provision of humanitarian aid to the local population.

The difference between the first and second generations results, on the one hand, from the subsidiary nature of such civilian missions in the mandates of the earlier peace-keeping operations, and, on the other hand, from the diversity of actors intervening in second-generation operations – civilian and military personnel sent by States, international organizations, and NGOs. Thus, the civilian aspects of peace-keeping operations are no longer limited to "non-military tasks entrusted to soldiers," to quote Brian Urquhart. Civilian personnel also participate, although there is no necessary connection between the relative size of the civilian and military components and the nature of the tasks entrusted to them.

Two categories of second-generation peace-keeping operation may be distinguished:

- military operations with humanitarian objectives, in which soldiers provide protection for humanitarian relief convoys and the personnel responsible for them, or actually deliver the aid themselves;
- hybrid operations, in which the civilian and military missions are complementary aspects of the operational mandate and of equal importance.

This classification allows us to distinguish a twofold evolution of the civilian tasks entrusted to peace-keeping operations: the evolution of the missions themselves and of the means employed to accomplish them.

2   Evolution of the missions

The extension of the civilian component of peace-keeping operations came about because the United Nations now envisages, beyond the cessation of hostilities, the creation of viable social conditions and legal and political systems which will guarantee the solutions achieved through conflict resolution.

For the United Nations, democratization, consolidated by free and fair elections, is the sign that internal political stability has been attained. However, as a result of the internal political and humanitarian situation in the States in which the Organization intervenes (often after many years of war), such democratization needs to be prepared for by sanitary, economic, administrative, and legal action.

The archetype for such missions was the Cambodian operation and the creation of the United Nations Transitional Authority in Cambodia (UNTAC), in which France played an important part. Together with the Supreme National Council,[2] UNTAC exercised a quasi-trusteeship over the State and its administration in order to create a politically neutral and socially stable environment. Although no operation set up since then has been as comprehensive, most peace-keeping operations deployed to promote democratization include, to some extent, action in favour of human rights, restoration of police and judicial systems, or aid to refugees.

Civil administration

The direct administration of a State by a United Nations mission is an intervention characteristic of the evolution of peace-keeping operations towards essentially civilian ends. Before such a mission was implemented on a large scale during the United Nations operation in Cambodia, there had only been more limited precedents: the role played for a short time by UNEF in assuring essential services including post and telecommunications in the Gaza strip, and the UNTEA mission in West Irian.

The stated aim of UNTAC was to ensure the neutrality of an administration reputed to be favourable to the regime in power so as to facilitate the organization and conduct of free and fair elections. The control over all departments likely to have an influence on the preparation or results of the elections was transferred to the Civil Administration Component of UNTAC, under the direction of a French administrative magistrate. In this way, control over foreign affairs, finance, defence, public security, and information were transferred to UNTAC with the agreement of the Supreme National Council.

UNTAC's control was exercised over both national and regional administrations. It assured neutrality at the national level by placing its own administrative officers in existing government departments. In the regions, which were all under the control of one or other of the four factions, the peace agreements gave the Secretary-General's Special Representative, Yasushi Akashi, unrestricted access to all activities and administrative records and allowed him to relocate or replace local administrative officers.

Administrative stability and, in the end, that of the country as a whole also depends on aid in setting up an effective civilian police force which respects human rights. For the Secretary-General's Special Representative in Haiti, Lakhdar Brahimini, the French police force is sufficiently experienced to be a model for training national police forces during peace-keeping operations.[3] French police and gendarmes participate in UN missions as much in the "civilian police" component of PKOs as in the training of national police forces. This was especially true in Haiti. France seconded around 100 police and gendarmes to the United Nations force, UNMIH II, and, in cooperation with American and Canadian personnel, set up a training programme for Haitian police officers once the police academy was reopened.

It should be noted that France has also sent police officers and gendarmes to Bosnia in similar circumstances.

Promotion and protection of human rights

If, until now, Cambodia remains the unique example of an all-out comprehensive action, the promotion and protection of human rights has become a constant aspect of peace-keeping operations. Thus, for example, as part of its activities in favour of human rights, the civil administration component of UNTAC was responsible for general supervision of human rights within all existing administrative systems, especially those responsible for law enforcement and the judicial system. The UN Centre for Human Rights has organized numerous training sessions for the civil components of peace-keeping operations (as in Mozambique), or even lent a hand in some operations by keeping communications open between the mission and specialized NGOs (as in Haiti).

France is known for the activism of its NGOs, especially the "French doctors" of *Médecins du Monde* and *Médecins sans Frontières*. During their interventions, these NGOs are frequently present at the same time as urgently deployed UN operations. While cooperation between them is the exception, according to the

NGOs,[4] the partnership between the International Civilian Mission in Haiti (MICIVIH) and one NGO, *Médecins du Monde* (MDM), underlines the value of such cooperation, which must increase as UN operations spread into the fields of "natural" interest of NGOs.

MICIVIH, a joint operation between the Organization of American States and the United Nations in Haiti since February 1993, was deployed after an OAS initiative to set up a civilian mission (OEA/DEMOC) in October 1991 after the coup against President Jean-Bertrand Aristide, to re-establish and strengthen constitutional democracy in Haiti. In addition to support for this operation from the United Nations, the two organizations began negotiations to set up a joint mission. The General Assembly took responsibility for UN involvement in an action in favour of human rights in its Resolution 47/20 B, on 20 April 1993. At the same time, UNMIH, a PKO authorized by the Security Council (Resolution 940) was entrusted with missions related to the organization of elections and keeping the peace.[5]

MICIVIH was entrusted with verification of "compliance with Haiti's international human rights obligations, with a view to making recommendations thereon, in order to assist in the establishment of a climate of freedom and tolerance propitious to the re-establishment of democracy in Haiti."[6] Before the legislative and presidential elections, MICIVIH was also mandated, in collaboration with UNMIH and the OAS election observation mission, to supervise respect for the freedom of expression and association and the vote itself.

The missions entrusted to MICIVIH were thus purely civilian. It was required to observe and report on violations of human rights and, through its presence, promote freedom of expression and opinion. In addition, as a "natural" complement to its mission, MICIVIH set up a medical and psychological assistance unit for the victims of torture, rape, and inhuman treatment. NGO action, in what was known as the MICIVIH/MDM medical unit, was funded by the French Ministry for Cooperation. The request for funds was made by MICIVIH for use by MDM.

Informal working agreements have been drawn up, including an agreement on the distribution and rationalization of medical assistance and a special agreement within MICIVIH for a medical clinic devoted to the victims of violations of human rights, to allow coordinated action. MICIVIH also undertook direct action in favour of victims of torture and inhuman treatment. On the one hand, during its enquiries into human rights violations, it undertook psychological care of individual victims, "recommending" patients to the medical unit. On the other hand, it rehabilitated the existing medical infrastructure, which had ceased treating patients for fear of reprisals, by setting up a network of local doctors and hospitals.

From its observations, the MICIVIH medical unit compiled reports which could be of use to the renewed judicial system or any *ad hoc* commission created for the recognition and indemnization of victims, despite the amnesty.

Such cooperation between an international mission and an NGO seems relatively exceptional. Most of the time their actions remain clearly distinct. On the other hand, in some cases, peace-keeping operations may be deployed with a view to improving the delivery of humanitarian aid, often by NGOs.

Finally, it should be noted that UN action in favour of human rights exceeds the bounds of peace-keeping operations. The UN Electoral Assistance Unit continues the work started in peace-keeping operations through its support for local offices and NGOs working in the human rights field.

Support for the local population

Support for the local population is many-faceted. It may include transporting supplies or free medical assistance (consultations, vaccinations, emergency transport by army health services) in regions where such services are non-existent. It may also include the reconstruction of roads and bridges, repairs to schools, houses and water supplies, as was the case for the French Engineers battalion stationed in Cambodia.

De-mining is a United Nations intervention priority for civilian populations. It takes numerous forms: de-mining itself, training local personnel, and awareness training for the local populace. In Cambodia, UNTAC, with heavy French involvement, was able to train 2,300 local de-miners. A national infrastructure, the Cambodian De-mining Centre, was set up to allow continued de-mining operations after the departure of the UN personnel in November 1993.

The complementary action of NGOs is particularly important in this domain, especially as concerns the organization of awareness campaigns on the human and economic consequences of these weapons. In France the efforts to raise public opinion have mainly been undertaken by Handicap International, which, in addition to its medical rehabilitation of victims of anti-personnel mines, has launched an information campaign on "the coward's war" and symbolic actions, such as the construction of a pyramid of shoes in Paris in September 1996, each shoe representing a mine victim.

Apart from UN operations, France has taken action to modify the international regime in this area. It has decided to announce a moratorium on the exportation of anti-personnel mines and was one of the first States to request the amendment of the 1980 Convention on prohibitions or restrictions on the use of certain conventional weapons which may be deemed to be excessively injurious or to have indiscriminate effects. This action has been doubled at the European level by the adoption of a common policy (10 April 1995) including the above points, *mutatis mutandis*, and deciding to contribute to funding for the Revision Conference for the 1980 Convention held in Geneva from 5 to 7 July 1995.

Electoral assistance

Present in the mandates of numerous peace-keeping operations,[7] electoral assistance has become, to various degrees, a constant aspect of UN operations. Since the creation of the electoral assistance unit in 1992, the United Nations have been involved in the electoral processes of 61 States.[8] All involvement is preceded by a resolution of the Security Council or the General Assembly. It takes three main forms: supervision, verification, and the organization and conduct of elections.

Election supervision

Election supervision has been undertaken only in the context of decolonization. It would be difficult to offer such assistance to a State as this would violate its sovereignty. In addition, this sort of assistance requires enormous material and human resources. It was used in Namibia, by UNTAG, for the election of representatives to its first Constituent Assembly just before Namibia's independence.

Verification of elections

In this approach, the United Nations certify the legitimacy of the conduct of elections. All aspects of the electoral process are verified: voter registration, civic education, the electoral campaign, equal access of political parties to the media, conduct of the election, vote counting and announcement of the results. This type of action requires a prolonged presence. ONUVEN, one of the first such missions, for example, was deployed in Nicaragua in August 1989 for the elections held in February 1990.

Organization and conduct of elections

This type of assistance is more complex and difficult for the United Nations to implement owing to the human and material means it requires. It has only really been attempted once, as part of the UN operation in Cambodia. The Paris Peace Agreements entrusted UNTAC with responsibility for "the organization and conduct of the elections."[9] This required the preparation of the whole range of rules necessary before elections can be held (drafting of the Electoral Law and the Code of Conduct regulating participation in the elections), the conduct of the electoral process (voter registration, registration of political parties, etc.), and the vote itself (conduct, counting, and announcement of the results). To give an idea of the size of such an operation, organization of the elections required 1,500 polling stations spread through 20 of the 21 provinces, plus 200 mobile polling stations, 1,400 international supervisors and 130 members of UN agencies, 47 international observers, and 1,700 independent observers. UNTAC was also the final electoral judge in that it was the body which received and resolved complaints.

3 Evolution of the means employed

Military operations with humanitarian objectives

It has already been shown how peace-keeping operations have progressively incorporated civilian aspects, involving more and more civilian personnel working side by side with military personnel. As the civilian missions take on a greater importance,[10] however, the actors entrusted with these missions have changed, in that military personnel sometimes fulfill civilian missions within the framework of peace-keeping operations. This is particularly true in the humanitarian field, the subject of this section.

Humanitarian concerns are taking a greater place within international organizations and have become a central aspect of the foreign policy of many States.[11] This awareness of humanitarian imperatives did not, however, come about as a result of the evolution of international law but rather through the means employed to ensure the respect for international humanitarian law.

Humanitarian action is the main role of NGOs and specialized UN institutions such as the Office of the High Commissioner for Refugees (UNHCR), which are often present in the field long before (and long after) the arrival of United Nations forces. In a number of troubled situations where such personnel and the local population were in danger, the Blue Helmets have been given a humanitarian mandate, as much to ensure the protection of the personnel in charge of the humanitarian action as to provide assistance directly, through force when necessary.

The Security Council has played a major role in this respect, through the adoption of resolutions which have progressively created a *link between humanitarian assistance and Chapter VII*. Resolution 688 (1991), in which the Council "insisted" that Iraq "allow immediate access" to humanitarian organizations, is an historic precedent, although its extent is limited. In reality, the Council was far from authorizing the use of force to accomplish its ends, and although it had qualified the internal situation in Iraq as a "threat to peace" in accordance with Chapter VII, this was stated to be due to the flood of refugees entering neighbouring countries. A further step was taken in 1992 with the adoption of Resolutions 770 and 794 on 13 August and 2 December, regarding Bosnia and Herzegovina and Somalia, respectively. In both cases the Security Council authorized Member States to use "all necessary means" to deliver humanitarian aid. This established a link between humanitarian action and coercive measures under Chapter VII.

Three of the operations set up by the United Nations in 1992 were expressly given humanitarian mandates, for the first time in the history of peace-keeping operations. They were UNPROFOR (United Nations Protection Force in the former Yugoslavia), UNOSOM (United Nations Operation in Somalia) and ONUMOZ (United Nations Operation in Mozambique). The first two will be dealt with here, due to the active French participation in them.

UNPROFOR
In former Yugoslavia, UNPROFOR was sent first to Croatia, in response to military concerns, to help put an end to a conflict between Serbs and Croatians in Croatia through interposition between the belligerents and the demilitarization of certain areas. It was with the extension of UNPROFOR to Bosnia and Herzegovina that humanitarian concerns began to play a large part in the mandate. At first, the mandate was limited to control of Sarajevo airport and control of all aid

transiting through it, as well as supervision of the numerous but short-lived cease-fires. The adoption of Security Council Resolution 770 (1992) began the incredible expansion of the Blue Helmets' humanitarian mission, by authorizing Member States to take "all measures necessary to facilitate in co-ordination with the United Nations the delivery by relevant United Nations humanitarian organizations and others of humanitarian assistance to Sarajevo and wherever needed in other parts of Bosnia and Herzegovina." In the end, this new mission was performed by UNPROFOR itself, under the authority of Security Council Resolution 776, 14 September 1992.

In 1993, UNPROFOR's mandate for the protection of the civilian population took on a new dimension. In response to intensifying attacks on a number of towns in Bosnia and Herzegovina in which the population from surrounding regions had taken refuge, the Security Council requested, in Resolution 824 of 6 May 1993, that six such towns, including Sarajevo, be protected from the danger of such attacks. Based on a French proposal, the Council decided to designate the towns and their environs as "safe areas." A "safe area" is defined as "a besieged area, with a precisely defined perimeter, placed under the protection of the United Nations, in which the delivery of humanitarian assistance is ensured and all acts of aggression banned."[12] In Resolution 836 of 3 June 1993, the Security Council again extended UNPROFOR's mandate to "deter attacks against the safe areas."

The "safe area" concept created new relationships between the military and humanitarian components entrusted, respectively, with protection and assistance missions. The concept itself is not new,[13] but the specificity of such zones, as they have been used since the end of the Cold War, is that security may be guaranteed by armed intervention.[14]

This evolution of UNPROFOR's mandate shows how the humanitarian element progressively became preponderant. From being ordered to protect Sarajevo airport and the foreign aid transiting through it, the force was led to escort humanitarian convoys, to fight local militias on occasion, and to then protect the security of the areas in which humanitarian assistance was being delivered.

UNOSOM

UNOSOM had a clearly humanitarian vocation. From the start, the mission was intended to remedy the humanitarian emergency unfolding in Somalia. The

Organization's intention in setting up a peace-keeping operation was to fortify the efforts of other UN humanitarian organizations whose action was being hindered by the serious ongoing unrest in Somalia. UNOSOM was thus given humanitarian missions, such as emergency aid, recovery and reconstruction, along with more traditional missions such as supervision of cease-fires, security, demobilization, and disarmament, as well as mediation and good offices in the peace process aimed at national reconciliation. Through Security Council Resolution 775 of 28 August 1992, the force's tasks were clarified. Units were required to "provide security at the port, escort convoys of relief supplies to distribution centres and protect the centres during distribution."[15] As with UNPROFOR, military means were employed to ensure delivery of humanitarian aid.

In the face of persistent violence, insecurity, and anarchy in the country, UNOSOM's mandate was extended a number of times to increase the protection of personnel, infrastructure, and equipment of the force itself, other UN organs, the International Committee of the Red Cross (ICRC), and other NGOs. The mandate permitted the use of force against armed groups threatening or attacking the infrastructure or personnel of these organizations. Numerous other tasks were given to the force, including maintenance of order and weapons control, so as to recreate secure conditions in Somalia. This evolution allows the same conclusion to be drawn as for UNPROFOR. Initially limited to the protection of personnel and relief convoys, UNOSOM progressively became a force entrusted with the security of all humanitarian assistance, especially when the cease-fire was repeatedly violated.

These two operations, UNPROFOR and UNOSOM, completed the evolution towards the strengthening of the means of action of UN forces in humanitarian matters.

The inclusion of major humanitarian missions in the mandates of peace-keeping operations was a major innovation. Even more remarkable was the fact that these missions included the protection by UN forces of the delivery of humanitarian assistance to populations in need (owing to obstruction by belligerents) as well as their direct protection from the effects of the hostilities.

Operation Turquoise

While it was not, strictly speaking, a peace-keeping operation, Operation Turquoise, in which France played a central role, certainly rates a mention. The major development was the increased emphasis placed on the humanitarian dimension of collective security. Faced with the inability of the United Nations Assistance Mission for Rwanda (UNAMIR) to fulfill its mission, the Security Council assented, in Resolution 929 of 22 June 1994, to a French proposal to resolve the impasse, deciding that "a multinational operation may be set up for humanitarian purposes in Rwanda until UNAMIR is brought up to the necessary strength" to accomplish its mandate. Accordingly, the Security Council received favourably "the offer by Member States (S/1994/734) to co-operate with the Secretary-General in order to achieve the objectives of the United Nations in Rwanda through the establishment of a temporary operation under national command and control aimed at contributing, in an impartial way, to the security and protection of displaced persons, refugees and civilians at risk in Rwanda ... Acting under Chapter VII of the Charter of the United Nations, the Council authorizes the Member States co-operating with the Secretary-General to conduct the operation referred to in paragraph 2 above using all necessary means to achieve the humanitarian objectives set out in subparagraphs 4 (*a*) and (*b*) of resolution 925 (1994)," in other words, "(*a*) Contribute to the security and protection of displaced persons, refugees and civilians at risk in Rwanda, including through the establishment and maintenance, where feasible, of secure humanitarian areas; and (*b*) Provide security and support for the distribution of relief supplies and humanitarian relief operations." This mission, the usefulness of which is now evident, was a success because it was carried out by élite troops with a precise mandate, dissuading any party to the conflict from trying to obstruct them.

Although it is still too early to make a final assessment of this evolution in the means employed towards the achievement of civilian objectives, a number of legal and political problems arising out of the expansion of UN mandates may already be identified. A number of lessons can be drawn from past experience, which may lead to improved efficiency and effectiveness of the close link which is growing between humanitarian and military action.

The military and the humanitarian: A controversial mix

First, it is interesting to note that most of the principal Security Council resolutions concerning the conflict in Somalia were adopted unanimously. Innovative decisions changing traditional UN practices in the peace-keeping field attracted little public objection from Security Council members.

Reasons for the interaction between military and humanitarian action

A number of different factors combine to explain the generalization of the link between humanitarian assistance and peace-keeping. First of all, humanitarian emergencies may cause conflicts, or may be an exacerbating factor. In some cases, the parties to a conflict have sought to provoke such emergency situations deliberately in order to attain their strategic goals. In the case of Bosnia and Herzegovina, the Secretary-General noted that "the infliction of hardship on civilians is actually a war aim as it leads to the desired movements of population from certain areas. Therefore there appears to be a predisposition to use force to obstruct relief supplies."[17] It is in this context that the Secretary-General and the Security Council have underlined the interaction between humanitarian assistance and the re-establishment of international peace and security. The inclusion of humanitarian tasks in the mandate of UN forces makes humanitarian action a new element in the management or resolution of essentially internal conflicts. Food aid given to demobilized combatants and humanitarian assistance given to populations no longer receiving support from their own State show how the humanitarian aspects of peace-keeping operations reinforce the general goal of a return to peace. The concept underlying this evolution of the mandates of UN operations is that of a more global approach to the concept of conflict itself, taking its causes and consequences into account and attempting to act upon them. The Secretary-General himself underlined the fact that "the second generation of peace-keeping is certain to involve not only military but also political, economic, social, humanitarian and environmental dimensions" and that they are "all in need of a unified and integrated approach."[17] These statements show clearly the United Nations' wish to enlarge the humanitarian vocation of peace-keeping operations in the medium to long term. Humanitarian action seems almost to have become an essential element of such operations, perhaps even overriding the traditional goal of peace-keeping.

This opening up of the role of the United Nations to include humanitarian action, not always clearly distinguished from its traditional mission of maintaining international peace and security, feeds upon diplomatic perceptions of the "right of humanitarian intervention." This results in some suspicion regarding such operations, because the application of this "right" (with all the precautions which must be taken with regard to this principle) sometimes results in armed interventions which go far beyond the simple distribution of medicine or food relief. In addition, the use of force leads ineluctably to abuse and accidents.

Unfortunately, the use of military means to support humanitarian action, or to protect the personnel supplying it, seems indispensable. This was especially the case in Somalia, a country overtaken by the anarchy of armed gangs and looters out of all control. The effectiveness of humanitarian assistance may thus be directly linked to the level of insecurity in the country.

Problems stemming from the interaction of military and humanitarian action

Whereas the NGO *Médecins sans Frontières* has vigorously criticized the excessive militarization of UN operations, notably in the humanitarian field in 1993 (i.e. Rwanda), the president of the ICRC, Cornelio Sommaruga, is more moderate in that he recognizes that recourse to military intervention in the humanitarian field is necessary, even indispensable. "In the context of the new collective security system which, under UN control, would take more direct account of the causes of human tragedy, the use of force remains possible as a last option in cases of extreme distress." Thus, the use of armed escorts should only be a temporary and exceptional remedy. He specifies, however, along with many other authors,[18] that it is imperative to "establish and preserve a fundamental distinction between the role of States and that of impartial humanitarian organizations."[19] They have two distinct functions. Merging them into a single process implemented by States through forceful means and in substitution for humanitarian organizations would politicize humanitarian action, placing it in contradiction with its philosophy of neutrality and impartiality.

In every peace-keeping operation, it is thus indispensable to preserve a humanitarian space guaranteeing the independence and neutrality of humanitarian action, clearly separate from any military action. Mixing humanitarian goals with military and political objectives renders the assistance unacceptable to the parties to the conflict and the victims for whom they are responsible. Peace-keeping operations with purely security and humanitarian goals cannot be maintained indefinitely. There must be a basic wish to resolve the conflict politically and implement the corresponding agreements. Even so, the effective complementarity of military and humanitarian action cannot be denied. UN interventions (or those by multinational forces under UN mandates) can contribute to the creation of a favourable environment for humanitarian action. In every conflict, it is in the interests of the victims that the respective roles of humanitarian organizations and the United Nations be clarified as soon as possible, and that effective collaboration be established between these institutions.

The Secretary-General has also noted the inherent political and material limits to such mixed operations, when referring to the conflict in former Yugoslavia. On 30 October 1994, he stated that "no mission can realistically use force in one part of the conflict zone and continue to act as a neutral humanitarian operation and impartial partner in another."[20] He recognized, in May 1995, that "UNPROFOR is almost paralysed by the nature and complexity of its mission, both humanitarian (protection of the delivery of assistance to the civilian population) and peace-keeping (enforcing respect, through armed action if necessary, of the safe areas and exclusion zones decreed by the Council)".[21]

In this way the links between humanitarian and military action lead to ambiguity. The need to distinguish carefully between peace-keeping operations and humanitarian action may be pointed out, but, in practice, the distinction is only possible if the two types of action are not implemented by the same actor.

One risk which flows from this combination may be the temptation for the intervening powers to hide political powerlessness, diplomatic blockage, or the absence of any active will to resolve the conflict durably behind humanitarian assistance. Humanitarian action must not become a substitute for political action and cannot, of itself, constitute a foreign policy.

In the light of the Yugoslavian and Somali experiences, the risks run by the troops in the field, the complexity and sheer size of the tasks to be completed, the uncertainty concerning the durability of results achieved, and the refusal of belligerents to seek compromise and peace put the validity of such operations in doubt and might lead some to believe it necessary to return to a more traditional concept of peace-keeping.

Prudence is thus required in considering the evolution of the new missions entrusted to peace-keeping operations. It should be remembered that, whichever option is considered – return to traditional mandates or the systematic integration of civilian aspects into the mandate of UN forces – one factor remains unchanged. The UN must be given the political and material means to carry out its missions. In any case, the strengthening of humanitarian action on the international scene and the current link between military and humanitarian action constitutes an unprecedented progress in the management of post–Cold War crises and conflicts, marking the increasing importance now placed upon the person in the processes of peace and development.

Notes

1. *Supplement to An Agenda for Peace*, 3 January 1995, para. 21.
2. The Supreme National Council was defined as "the unique legitimate body and source of authority in which, throughout the transitional period, the sovereignty, independence and unity of Cambodia are enshrined" (Art. 3 of the Agreement on a Comprehensive Settlement). It represented Cambodia in all foreign relations, including those with the United Nations, and was composed of members representing all of the existing currents of opinion.
3. "Les Missions des Nations Unies en Haïti: Mode d'emploi pour une Mission de maintien de la paix" [The UN Missions in Haiti: practical guide for a PKO], in Yves Daudet (ed.), *La crise d'Haïti (1991–1996)* Cahiers internationaux no. 12, CEDIN Paris I (Paris: Montchrestien, 1996), p. 60.
4. Interview with Florence Trintignac and Thierry Choubrac of *Médecins du Monde*.
5. See Daudet (ed.), *La crise d'Haïti (1991–1996)*.
6. General Assembly Resolution 47/20 B, 20 April 1993.
7. Namely, UNTAG (Namibia, 1989), ONUCA (Central America, 1989), ONUVEH (Haiti, 1990), ONUSAL (El Salvador, 1993), MINURSO (Western Sahara, 1991), UNAVEM II (Angola, 1991), UNTAC (Cambodia, 1992), UNOMSA (South Africa, 1992), UNOVER (Eritrea, 1993), ONUMOZ (Mozambique, 1992) and UNMIH (Haiti, 1993); dates correspond to the time the Security Council defined the electoral mandate.
8. Boutros Boutros-Ghali, *1995 Annual Report on the Activities of the Organization* (New York: United Nations, 1995), para. 964.
9. Agreement on a Comprehensive Political Settlement of the Cambodia Conflict, Paris, 23 October 1991, Art. 13 and Annexe 1, section D.
10. "The Organization must find the means to link humanitarian action and the protection of human rights to peacemaking, peace-keeping and peace-building operations." Boutros Boutros-Ghali, *1993 Annual Report on the Activities of the Organization*, quoted in Olivier Corten and Pierre Klein, "Action humanitaire et chapitre VII: la redéfinition du mandat et des moyens d'action des forces des Nations Unies" [Humanitarian Action and Chapter VII: redefining the mandates and means of action of UN forces], *Annuaire français de droit international*, 1993, p. 105.

11. It is worth noting here the resolutions adopted by the General Assembly after a French proposal (the Kouchner–Bettati doctrine on "the right of humanitarian intervention," which, of course, is a right only in name), A/Res/43/131 on humanitarian assistance to victims of natural disasters and similar emergency situations, 8 December 1988; and A/Res/45/100, which takes up the proposal to establish "relief corridors" in emergencies to facilitate the delivery of aid, 14 December 1990.

12. French memorandum on safe areas (*zones de sécurité*), UN Doc. S/25800, para. 1.

13. The Geneva Conventions designate "hospital zones and localities," "hospital and safety zones and localities," and "neutralized zones." For more details see Maurice Torelli, "Les zones de sécurité," *Revue générale de droit international public* no. 4,1995, pp. 788–847.

14. It should be noted that numerous variants were created during the Yugoslavian conflict: UN Protected Areas (UNPAs), established in Croatia under the Vance plan for deployment of UNPROFOR (Security Council Resolution 743, 21 February 1992); "pink zones" adjacent to the UNPAs, also protected under Security Council Resolution 762, 30 June 1992; "no-fly zones" (ban on military flights in the airspace) over the Republic of Bosnia and Herzegovina (Security Council Resolutions 781, 9 October 1992, and 816, 31 March 1993); "safe areas" as such, established around Srebrenica (Resolution 819, 17 April 1993), Sarajevo, Gorazde, Zepa, Tuzla, and Bihac (Resolution 824, 6 May 1993), whose security could be ensured by force under Resolution 836 of 4 June 1993; and finally "heavy weapon exclusion zones" around Sarajevo and Gorazde.

15. Secretary-General's Report on the situation in Somalia, S/24480, 24 August 1992, para. 25.

16. Report by the Secretary-General in accordance with Security Council Resolution 52 (1992), S/24000, 26 May 1992, para. 18.

17. Boutros Boutros-Ghali, *1993 Annual Report on the Activities of the Organization*, para. 6.

18. See, for example, Jean-Christophe Rufin, "Les pièges de l'humanitaire" [The traps of humanitarian action], *Revue des deux mondes*, June 1993, pp. 129–39.

19. Cornelio Sommaruga, "Action humanitaire et opérations de maintien de la paix" [Humanitarian action and peace-keeping operations], *Revue internationale de la Croix-Rouge*, 801, May–June 1993, p. 266.

20. *New York Times*, 30 October 1994.

21. *Le Monde*, 26 May 1995.

CONCLUSION

Brigitte Stern

Undoubtedly, a number of obvious conclusions may be drawn from a reading of the contributions making up the body of this work, which have presented the varying and impassioned relations between France and peace-keeping operations from a range of perspectives: political, legal, financial, and humanitarian. Even so, it may be of use to highlight the salient aspects of these relations.

On the internal level in France, one might question whether France really employs the parliamentary system when dealing with issues involving the use of force within the UN framework and participation in peace-keeping operations. The fact is that in France the President of the Republic has a *discretionary power* regarding participation in peace-keeping operations, even if Parliament can exercise some control *a posteriori* through its vote on the funding necessary for such operations. When France's strong involvement in the system of peace-keeping operations is taken into account, it becomes clear that this seriously undermines the nation's democratic control over the deployment of French soldiers outside French territory.

On the international level, France was reluctant at first regarding the "Chapter VI and-a-half" innovations which led to peace-keeping operations being set up by the General Assembly in contravention of the institutional balance provided for in the Charter, giving the five permanent members a primordial role in maintaining peace through their participation in the work of the Security Council. In contrast, France is now heavily involved in peace-keeping operations, especially since the fall of the Berlin Wall allowed a return to basics, to the original text of San Francisco, which conferred on the Security Council "primary responsibility for the maintenance of international peace and security."

France's involvement manifests itself at all levels. As regards *doctrinal reflection* on peace-keeping operations, France has made the specific contribution of the concept of "humanitarian intervention," and more recently, that of "overseas force projection."

As for its *financial contribution*, France has effectively provided 7.62 per cent of the peace-keeping operations budget, even though its share of the ordinary budget is only 6.4 per cent.

Of course, the most visible aspect of this France's participation is the *human contribution* to peace-keeping operations. A few statistics show the strength of French involvement: overall, 15,127 French soldiers have served with UNIFIL since March 1978, while 6,400 men served with UNTAC between March 1992 and November 1993. The French involvement in UNPROFOR from February 1992 to December 1995, however, broke all records, with a total of 44,551 soldiers serving. Given that the missions carried out by such operations are often dangerous, requiring soldiers to keep a non-existent peace, such a large involvement inevitably signifies a heavy toll of dead and wounded. That is the price France is prepared to pay to retain its rank as a permanent member of the Security Council and a defender of the fundamental values of international society, respect for human rights and humanitarian law, democracy, and peace.

APPENDIX I

(a) French foreign operations past and present, as at 26 March 1996

Period	Country or zone	Acronym	Means employed	Observations
Since 06/48	Egypt–Israel–Jordan–Syria–Lebanon	UNTSO	18 men (10 army)	United Nations Truce Supervision Organization
03/78	South Lebanon	HIPPO-CAMPE	1,500 (army)	Participation in United Nations Interim Force in Lebanon (UNIFIL)
Since 03/78	South Lebanon	UNIFIL	530 (army)	Interposition mission
Since 04/91	Iraq/Kuwait	UNIKOM	15 (10 army)	United Nations Iraq–Kuwait Observation Mission
Since 05/91	El Salvador	ONUSAL	15 (gendarmes)	United Nations Observer Mission in EL Salvador
Since 10/91	Western Sahara	MINURSO	30 (19 army)	United Nations Mission for the Referendum in Western Sahara

Period	Country or zone	Acronym	Means employed	Observations
10/91–02/92	Cambodia	UNAMIC	114 (105 army)	United Nations Advance Mission in Cambodia
02/92–12/95	Former Yugoslavia	UNPROFOR	6,800 (army, navy, air force)	United Nations Protection Force
03/92–11/93	Cambodia	UNTAC	1,470 (1,200 army)	United Nations Transitional Authority in Cambodia
Since 05/93	Somalia	UNOSOM II	1,100 (army)	United Nations Operation in Somalia
31/05/94–26/05/95	Cambodia	UNCONSMIL	1 (army)	Military advisor to the Representative of the UN Secretary General
18/06/94–26/05/95	Rwanda	Turquoise	2,256 (army)	Humanitarian assistance under UN Security Council Resolution 929
Since 21/09/94	Haiti	UNMIH	2 (army)	United Nations Mission in Haiti
Since 17/10/94	Georgia (former USSR)	UNOMIG	3 (army)	United Nations Observer Mission in Georgia
Since 16/12/94	USA	UNMIRE	1	Intelligence officer in the peace-keeping operations Situation Room, New York
Since 22/03/95	Angola	UNAVEM III	8 observers 12 de-miners	United Nations Angola Verification Mission; De-mining Training Mission

(b) French military personnel in foreign operations on behalf of the United Nations

Total numbers of French military personnel who have participated in:

UNIFIL	since 03/1978	15,127
UNTAC	03/1992–11/1993	6,400
UNPROFOR	02/1992–12/1995	44,551

APPENDIX II

French armed forces killed and
wounded in the course of United
Nations peace-keeping operations

LEBANON / *UNIFIL* : SINCE 03/1978															

	DEATHS				SERIOUSLY WOUNDED				LIGHTLY WOUNDED				TOTAL WOUNDED			
	x	y	z	tot.	x	y	z	tot.	x	y	z	tot.	x	y	z	tot.
Total				15												42

SAUDI ARABIA / *DAGUET* : 09/1990 - 06/1991															

	DEATHS				SERIOUSLY WOUNDED				LIGHTLY WOUNDED				TOTAL WOUNDED			
	x	y	z	tot.	x	y	z	tot.	x	y	z	tot.	x	y	z	tot.
Total				4												39

IRAQ / *UNIKOM* : 04/1991 - 12/1995															

	DEATHS				SERIOUSLY WOUNDED				LIGHTLY WOUNDED				TOTAL WOUNDED			
	x	y	z	tot.	x	y	z	tot.	x	y	z	tot.	x	y	z	tot.
Total				3												6

THE FORMER YUGOSLAVIA / *UNPROFOR* : 02/1992 - 12/1995

	DEATHS				SERIOUSLY WOUNDED				LIGHTLY WOUNDED				TOTAL WOUNDED			
	x	y	z	tot.	x	y	z	tot.	x	y	z	tot.	x	y	z	tot.
From combat action				19				36				228				264
Traffic Accidents				21				21				113				134
Service Accidents				10				19				121				140
Self - wounding				2								4				4
Sickness				1				1				44				45
Total				53				77				510				587

CAMBODIA / *UNTAC* : 03/1992 - 11/1993

	DEATHS				SERIOUSLY WOUNDED				LIGHTLY WOUNDED				TOTAL WOUNDED			
	x	y	z	tot.	x	y	z	tot.	x	y	z	tot.	x	y	z	tot.
From combat action					1	3	1	5					1	3	1	5
Traffic Accidents			2	2			4	4			2	2			6	6
Service Accidents						1	4	5	1	1	7	9	1	2	11	14
Sickness							5	5				3			8	8
Total				2	1	4	14	19	1	1	12	14	2	5	26	33

SOMALIA / *UNOSOM* : 12/1992 - 12/1995

	DEATHS				SERIOUSLY WOUNDED				LIGHTLY WOUNDED				TOTAL WOUNDED			
	x	y	z	tot.	x	y	z	tot.	x	y	z	tot.	x	y	z	tot.
Total				0												3

RWANDA / *TURQUOISE* : 18/06/1994 - 30/09/1994

	DEATHS				SERIOUSLY WOUNDED				LIGHTLY WOUNDED				TOTAL WOUNDED			
	x	y	z	tot.	x	y	z	tot.	x	y	z	tot.	x	y	z	tot.
From combat action								2								2
Service Accidents								3								3
Sickness				1												
Total				1				5								5

APPENDIX III

Relevant articles of the French Constitution of 1958

Article 5: (par. 2) "[The President] shall be the guarantor of national independence, the integrity of the territory and the respect of ... treaties."

Article 15: "The President is the Commander in Chief of the Armed Forces and chairs higher national defence councils and committees."

Article 20: "The government shall determine and conduct national policy. The Armed Forces shall be at its disposal ..."

Article 21: "The Prime Minister directs the conduct of government affairs and is responsible for national defence ..."

Article 35: "Declarations of War shall be authorized by Parliament."

Article 52: "The President of the Republic shall negotiate and ratify treaties. He is to be kept informed of all negotiations likely to lead to the conclusion of international agreements not requiring ratification."

Article 53: "Peace treaties, commercial treaties, treaties or agreements concerning international organization, those which involve the State in financial obligations, modify the provisions of the law, concern personal status or involve the cession, exchange or addition of territory may be ratified or approved only by virtue of a law. They take effect only after having been ratified or approved. No cession, exchange or addition of territory is valid without the consent of the populations concerned."

Source: A. Trentschler's Constitutional Law Resource (http://www.econ.uni-hamburg.de/law/)

BIBLIOGRAPHY

United Nations documents

Boutros-Ghali, Boutros, *An Agenda for Peace*. UN document A/47/277 – S/24111. New York: United Nations, 17 June 1992.

———, *Supplement to An Agenda for Peace*. UN document A/50/60 – S/1995/1. New York: United Nations, 3 January 1995.

———, *Annual Report on the Activities of the Organization*. New York: United Nations, 1993 and 1995.

French *aide-mémoire* in response to *An Agenda for Peace*. UN document A/48/403/Add.1, S/26450/Add.1. New York: United Nations, 28 July 1993.

French *aide-mémoire* in response to *Supplement to An Agenda for Peace*. UN document A/50/869, S/1996/71. New York: United Nations, 30 January 1995.

French official documents

Lanxade, J., "Orientations pour la conception, la préparation, la planification, le commandement et l'emploi des forces françaises dans les opérations militaires fondées sur une résolution du Conseil de sécurité des Nations Unies." Letter from Admiral Lanxade on France's military doctrine for peace-keeping operations. *Objectif 21, Revue du commandement, de la doctrine et de l'entraînement*, 1995/1.

Livre blanc sur la défense, preface by E. Balladur (Prime Minister) and F. Léotard (Defence Minister). UGE 10/18, 1994.

Raimond, J.-B. (rapporteur), *La politique d'intervention dans les conflits*. Information report no. 150 in the series *Les documents d'information*, Assemblée Nationale, Commission des affaires étrangères, 23 February 1995.

Trucy, François, "Rapport général sur le projet de loi des finances," Sénat no. 56, T.III-An. 43, 24 November 1992.

———, "Rapport au Premier Ministre: Participation de la France aux opérations de maintien de la paix." February 1994, mimeo.

Books and journal articles

Coicaud, Jean-Marc, "Les Nations Unies en Somalie: entre maintien et imposition de la paix." *Le Trimestre du Monde* 1, 1994: 96–134.

Corten, Olivier, and Pierre Klein, Action humanitaire et Chapitre VII: la rédéfinition du mandat et des moyens d'action des forces des Nations Unies." *Annuaire français de droit international*, 1993: 105–30.

Cot, Jean, *Dernière guerre balkanique? Ex-Yougoslavie: témoignage, analyses, perspectives.* Paris: Harmattan/FED, 1996.

Daudet, Yves, "Rapport introductif" aux Rencontres internationales de l'Institut d'études politiques d'Aix-en-Provence de 1991, organisées avec le concours du Centre d'information des Nations Unies à Paris. In *Aspects du système des Nations Unies dans le cadre de l'idée d'un nouvel ordre mondial.* Paris: Pédone, 1992.

———, "Rapport introductif" aux Rencontres internationales de l'Institut d'études politiques d'Aix-en-Provence de 1992, organisées avec le concours du Centre d'information des Nations Unies à Paris. In *Actualité des conflits internationaux.* Paris: Pédone, 1993.

———, "La restauration de l'État, nouvelle mission des Nations Unies?." In *Les Nations Unies et la reconstruction de l'État.* Paris: Pédone, 1995.

———, "Les Nations Unies et les évolutions du contenu du maintien de la paix." *Bulletin du Centre d'Information des Nations Unies à Paris*, special issue for the 50th anniversary of the United Nations, 1995.

———, "Les particularismes juridiques de la crise d'Haïti." In *La crise d'Haïti (1991–1996).* Cahiers internationaux no. 12, CEDIN Paris I. Paris: Montchrestien, 1996, pp. 29–46.

———, "Le droit au développement politique et le rôle des Nations Unies." In *Mélanges Bedjaoui*, Paris: UNESCO, forthcoming.

Ekwall-Vebelhart, Barbara, and Andreï Raevsky, *Disarmament and Conflict Resolution. Managing Arms in Peace Processes: Croatia and Bosnia Herzegovina.* New York/Geneva: UNIDIR, 1996.

Fondation pour les études de défense [FED], *Opérations des Nations Unies: leçons de terrain, Cambodge, Somalie, Rwanda, ex-Yougoslavie.* Paris: La Documentation française, collection "Perspectives stratégiques," 1995.

Ghebali, Victor-Yves, "Le développement des opérations de maintien de paix de l'ONU depuis de la fin de la guerre froide." *Le Trimestre du Monde* 4, 1992: 67–85.

Guillot, Philippe, "France, peacekeeping and humanitarian intervention." *International Peacekeeping*, Spring 1994: 30–43.

Keller, Gabriel, "La France et le Conseil de sécurité." *Le Trimestre du Monde* 4, 1992: 41–51.

Lafon, J.P., "Les Nations Unies et la prévention des conflits engendrés par les grands problèmes de société." In *Actualité des conflits internationaux, Rencontres internationales de l'IEP d'Aix en Provence*. Paris: Pédone, 1993, pp. 61–7.

Lewin, André (ed.), *La France et l'ONU depuis 1945*. Paris: Arléa-Corlet, 1995.

Macleod, Alex, "La France: à la recherche du leadership international." *Relations internationales et stratégiques* 19, Autumn 1995: 69–80.

Morillon, Philippe, *Paroles de soldat*. Paris: Balland, 1993.

———, *Croire et oser. Chroniques de Sarajevo*. Paris: Grasset, 1993.

Rufin, Jean-Christophe, "Les pièges de l'humanitaire." *Revue des deux mondes*, June 1993: 129–39.

Schricke, C, "Article 17 § 1 & 2." In J.P. Cot and A. Pellet, *La Charte des Nations Unies, Commentaire article par article*. Paris: Economica, 1991, pp.355–72.

Smouts, Marie-Claude, *La France et l'ONU*. Paris: Presses de la Fondation nationale des sciences politiques, 1979.

———, *L'ONU et la guerre. La diplomatie en kaki*. Brussels: Complexe, 1994.

———, "France and the United Nations system." In C. Alger, G. Lyons, and J. Trent (eds), *The United Nations System: Policies of the Member States*. Tokyo: United Nations University Press, 1995, pp. 186–230.

———, *Les organisations internationales*. Paris: Armand Colin, 1995.

Sommaruga, Cornelio, "Action humanitaire et opérations de maintien de la paix" [Humanitarian action and peace-keeping operations]. *Revue internationale de la Croix-Rouge*, 801, May–June 1993: 260–7.

Stern, Brigitte, "La sécurité collective: historique, bilan, perspectives." In *Sécurité collective et crises internationales*. Paris: SGDN, La Documentation française, 1994, pp. 145–73.

———, "L'évolution du rôle des Nations Unies dans le maintien de la paix et de la sécurité internationales." In *Le droit international comme langage des relations internationales*, Proceedings of the United Nations Congress on Public International Law, New York, 13–17 March 1995 (La Haye: Kluwer, 1996), pp. 58–64.

Stern, Brigitte (ed.), *Les aspects juridiques de la crise et de la guerre du Golfe*. Paris: Montchrestien, 1991.

Tardy, T., *La France et l'ONU, 50 ans de relations contrastées*. Regards sur l'actualité 215, November 1995. Paris: La Documentation française, pp. 3–23.

Tavernier, P., *Les Casques bleus*. Paris: P.U.F., 1996 (coll. Que sais-je?).

Torelli, Maurice, "Les missions humanitaires de l'armée française." *Revue de défense nationale*, March 1993: 65–78.

———, "Les zones de sécurité." *Revue générale de droit international public* no. 4, 1995: 788–847.

Weckel, P. "L'application du Chapitre VII de la Charte." *Annuaire français de droit international*, 1991: 165–202.

CONTRIBUTORS

Yves Daudet is Professor of International Law at the University of Paris I, Panthéon-Sorbonne, and a member of the Centre de droit international de Paris I (CEDIN Paris I.)

Philippe Morillon is a French army general. He commanded UNPROFOR from 1992 to 1993. In 1994-95 he was a Commander in the Rapid Reaction Force (*Force de réaction rapide*).

Marie-Claude Smouts is Research Director at the National Centre for Scientific Research (CERI, Centre for International Research and Studies) and Professor at the Institute of Political Studies in Paris.

Brigitte Stern is Professor of International Law at the University of Paris I, Panthéon-Sorbonne, and Director of the CEDIN Paris I. In February 1995 she was a visiting scholar at the UNU in Tokyo.

Sophie Albert assisted the authors in gathering the source material. She is a post-graduate student at the University of Paris I, Panthéon-Sorbonne, and a member of the CEDIN Paris I, and was a visiting scholar at the UNU in Tokyo for three months in 1995.

David Boyle translated this book from the French. He is a post-graduate student at the University of Paris II, Panthéon-Assas.

Olivier Deneve contributed to the completion of the chapter on the civil aspects of PKOs, and to the elaboration of the index. He is a post-graduate student at the University of Paris I, Panthéon-Sorbonne, and a member of the CEDIN Paris I.

Marie-Christine Poussin contributed to the completion of the chapter on the civil aspects of PKOs, and to the elaboration of the index. She is a post-graduate student at the University of Paris I, Panthéon-Sorbonne, and a member of the CEDIN Paris I.

Cedric Sylvestre is a researcher at the CEDIN, Paris I. He helped with the index and with editing.

Mandy Macdonald carried out the editing of the English version of the book for the United Nations University Press. She is a freelance editor and researcher specializing in development, gender, and human rights issues.

INDEX